高等职业教育“十四五”系列教材 汽车专业

汽车专业英语

主　编　潘天堂　陈　新
副主编　郑利峰
参　编　熊金凤　王秀梅
　　　　张红党　岳兴莲

U0361320

南京大学出版社

图书在版编目(CIP)数据

汽车专业英语 / 潘天堂，陈新主编. —南京：南京大学出版社，2022.1

ISBN 978-7-305-24134-5

Ⅰ. ①汽… Ⅱ. ①潘… ②陈… Ⅲ. ①汽车工程—英语—高等职业教育—教材 Ⅳ. ①U46

中国版本图书馆 CIP 数据核字(2020)第 265589 号

出版发行 南京大学出版社
社　　址 南京市汉口路 22 号　　　邮　　编 210093
出 版 人 金鑫荣

书　　名 汽车专业英语
主　　编 潘天堂 陈 新
责任编辑 吕家慧　　　编辑热线 025-83597482

照　　排 南京开卷文化传媒有限公司
印　　刷 丹阳兴华印务有限公司
开　　本 787×1092 1/16 印张 10.25 字数 224 千
版　　次 2022 年 1 月第 1 版 2022 年 1 月第 1 次印刷
ISBN 978-7-305-24134-5
定　　价 39.80 元

网　　址：http://www.njupco.com
官方微博：http://weibo.com/njupco
微信服务号：njuyuexue
销售咨询热线：(025)83594756

---

* 版权所有，侵权必究
* 凡购买南大版图书，如有印装质量问题，请与所购图书销售部门联系调换

前　言

本书以培养学生阅读和翻译汽车专业英语资料能力为主要目标，内容丰富，涉及汽车文化、汽车历史、汽车名企、汽车机械构造、汽车电气与电子控制、汽车先进技术、汽车排故、汽车现代检测技术、汽车保险、汽车营销、汽车驾驶、汽车推介、混合动力、电动汽车等，每个单元包括课文、词汇、复习提问和全文翻译，并配有扩展英文视频材料，课后新词均注有音标，便于学习，书后附有词汇表、汽车英文标牌，常用英文缩写等。所选内容既是对专业知识的英文回顾，也是对专业其他课程的扩展与补充，汽车检测与维修、汽车电子技术及汽车营销专业均可根据自身特点选用部分内容教学。

本书针对性较强，针对高、中等职业技术学院学生的学习特点，在选题上注重将科技与趣味相结合，将故事与总结相结合，将科技与人文相结合，将专业课程与工作实际要求相结合，将科普性与英文学习相结合，避免过于专业性的内容表达。

本书由潘天堂与陈新担任主编，郑利锋担任副主编，参加编写工作的还有熊金凤、王秀梅、张红党、岳兴莲等。

本书内容均摘自英文原版材料并经过认真的精简、缩编与校对，但由于编者水平有限，难免有不妥之处，恳请广大读者批评指正。

编　者

2021 年 4 月

Contents

Unit 1

Living in an Automobile Culture

扫码获取
扩展视频

Fig. 1 - 1 steam-driven carriage

People defend using automobiles instead of bicycles for traveling short distances by saying that bicycling is too dangerous or too difficult, ignoring the danger and difficulties brought about by the car. They pretend that car travel is no more expensive than the cost of filling the gasoline tank, thus ignoring the long hours they spend working to make payments on the car and its insurance. They ignore or deny the air pollution problems caused by autos, or they assume that the car protects them from exhaust fumes. (A recent study has found that the air is more polluted inside the vehicle than outside.) One know it all on the Web suggested that auto exhaust was now so clean that it couldn't be used to commit suicide! They ignore or accept as normal the health problems caused by their sedentary behavior, explaining that the ability of cyclists to get to work by bike comes from super human ability. And they desperately deny that global warming exists or that man has caused it because they don't wish to change their own behavior. In fact, even those motorists who recognize that global warming is a real problem are still waiting for someone else to solve that problem.

How did people become so dependent on motorized transportation? If we believe television and movies, every American family before the car had a horse and wagon or had horses and saddles for everyone. But this is just our car culture projected backwards. It took too much time and trouble to feed and care for a horse every day, (In the Westerns, the horse can magically travel for days without food.) so most people lived in towns where they could walk to all their destinations. Walking long distances was not a rare event and was seen as an enjoyable activity. Some people maintain that we are so dependent on automobiles because it is modern times or because of our affluence. However, the rest of the world has never become as auto dependent as we are. In Europe, where wages are as high as in the US, automobiles are involved in less than half of the trips in every country. Those who wish to deny this say, "Europe is smaller than the US, and people have shorter distances to travel." The first statement is not true unless we include Alaska, and the second statement is true because people in Europe generally don't choose to drive 50 miles to work. In any event, over half of the trips in the US are for distances of less than five miles.

In the past, the people who were dependent on vehicles were the wealthy. Even in cultures with no vehicles, it was often considered wrong for the king's sacred feet to touch the ground, and he was constantly fed, bathed, and otherwise attended to by women, so he became a fat, helpless, unhealthy, and short-lived child. Obviously, the intent was to cripple him as quickly as possible and to keep him as dependent as possible. In today's culture, a similar effort exists to make the consumer dependent. There's not much profit to be made of the healthy, self-reliant individual who can solve his own problems. I find I can cook an excellent meal for myself from scratch within 30 minutes, and while doing other work, at a cost of not much more than a dollar. Yet, many people are absolutely dependent on heat-and-serve food or restaurants, solutions that cost much more, take more time, and don't taste as good.

Fig. 1-2 Ford T-model car

But transportation dependency can lead to even larger profits. Henry Ford believed in America in which each family or person would own a car. At the same time, he was absolutely opposed to the use of streetcars, even to the point of insisting on not doing business with any company that received or shipped goods using their services. (Freight traffic on the streetcar lines was a good source of profit before the depression.) What was so wrong with streetcars? Were they inconvenient and expensive? Having spent the first ten years of my life in a city of streetcars, I can report that they were fun to travel on and not nearly the problem of an automobile. There was not the pollution and noise of the buses that replaced them. (Buses have improved since then.) It's true that we had to walk to the streetcar, but we could also get off right at our destination instead of making the long walk from the parking garage. It cost less to take a streetcar than to pay the parking fees. In fact, the cities have finally realized that their costs are lower when people leave the car at home. However, people who leave their automobiles at home reduce the profits of the automotive companies, and they don't burn gasoline or use tires—that's why automobile, gasoline, and auto tire companies conspired to destroy the streetcar lines.

Nowadays, when people say a car is a necessity, they are really saying that our society has been straining to make it a necessity. The little local businesses have largely dried up and are continuing to disappear due to people's willingness to drive five miles to save a nickel. Indeed, many people prefer to drive the extra five miles even if the price is no lower. The old winding roadways with their gradual grades and low speeds have been replaced with steep, fast, freeway type roads because people want to drive that five miles a little more impatiently every year. Each year the roadway looks a little more like a race track, and each year it takes a little more courage to become a cyclist.

People insist that they enjoy driving, but I wonder what kind of pleasure they are having. Some drivers spend their time cussing to themselves or yelling and screaming at everyone on the road. I can spot these motorists when I can't hear them because they will break a couple of laws and nearly kill me to pass my bike when I am less than fifty feet from a red light. One three lane section of road near my parents' home winds up a steep mountainside before turning into a two lane. This short section has become a desperate race track, with motorists making the sharp, blind turns at speeds 10 mph above the speed limit in order to be the first one up the hill. This driving behavior very much reminds me of walking between classes in junior high school, with all the kids pushing and shoving each other; it was chaos then, it is chaos now, and it's the same people. I have the suspicion that if these people really enjoyed driving that they would be willing to take their time and not endanger themselves and others.

It's very hard arguing with people who have brainwashed themselves into making a luxury into a necessity. Having redefined their lives to fit within an automobile world, they now insist that it's impossible to live without a car. They ask, "How could I otherwise make the 100 mile round trip to work?" Well, they could live very comfortably on a job that pays less than the cost of a daily 100 mile car trip. They could enjoy the extra time, too. "How could I get all the kids to school?" They have legs, don't they? "How could they get to school in the rain?" I walked to school for 15 years, and I can't remember one time when rain was a major problem. "How can we carry home groceries and other packages?" You have to use a two ton vehicle every single day because you get groceries once a month? At any rate, not owning a car does not lead to instant starvation and self deprivation, although they prefer to think that it does. In fact, they will find themselves with extra money and time, and—if they commute by walking or cycling—better health.

If someone asked me to give up riding the bike, what would my excuses be? I'd say I didn't want to miss the fresh morning air, the singing of the birds, the great feeling of being alive, the trees and flowers along the way, and the stars at night. Why would anyone want to ride around sealed up? I would also sorely miss the good exercise, as it takes 60 miles per week by bike to get the recommended amount. While spending the same amount of time walking would be almost as good, it would not take me to work or out into the country for a pleasant trip. And if I was forced to buy a car to make up for that transportation lack, I would have to find a higher paying job living somewhere I didn't want to live.

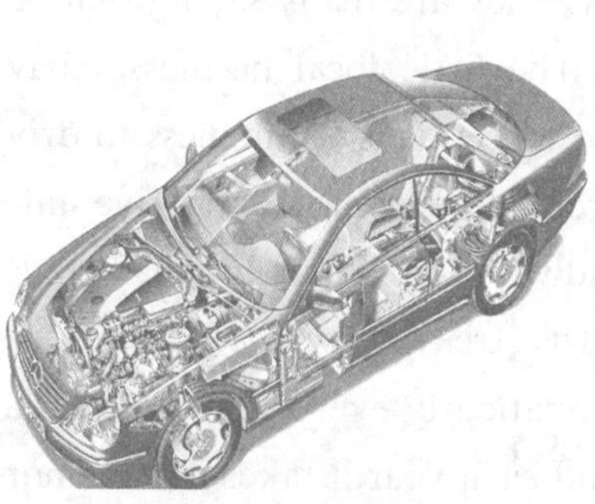
Fig. 1 - 3 modern cars

I admit that not everyone will ever be converted. Even if every expert acknowledges that global warming is real, even if every doctor tells his patients that they need more exercise, even if city streets are closed to cars, even if speed are reduced to 25 mph everywhere, and even if the cost of owning a car becomes exorbitant from gasoline taxes, parking fees, and other taxes, the American public is going to continue to identify with and to polish their automobiles. There is no way that something as humble, as practical, as convenient as a bicycle can win their hearts. The warmest spot in people's hearts will always be for that huge, fin covered, gas guzzling, shocking pink, 1959 Caddy. And they will forever be angry at us for taking their fun away. But it's long past time that the human race grew up and started acting like responsible people. Those of us who are mature and responsible have to fight through all of their crap and change the way the world is run, or our grandkids won't have a world.

NEW WORDS

defend	[dɪˈfend]	*vt.*	拒绝承认
pretend	[prɪˈtend]	*vt.*	假装
ignore	[ɪgˈnɔː]	*vt.*	忽视
sedentary	[ˈsedntri]	*adj.*	久坐的
desperately	[ˈdespərətlɪ]	*adv.*	极度地

motorist	[ˈməʊtərɪst]	*n.*	开汽车的人
destination	[ˌdestɪˈneɪʃən]	*n.*	目的地
wagon	[ˈwæɡən]	*n.*	四轮马车
saddle	[ˈsædl]	*n.*	鞍,鞍状物
cripple	[ˈkrɪpl]	*vt.*	使陷于瘫痪
streetcar	[ˈstritˌkɑr]	*n.*	有轨电车
freight	[freɪt]	*n.*	货运列车
garage	[ˈɡærɑːʒ]	*n.*	车库
tire	[ˈtaɪə]	*n.*	配用轮胎
roadway	[ˈrəʊdweɪ]	*n.*	道路
conspire	[kənˈspaɪə(r)]	*vt.*	共谋
cyclist	[ˈsaɪklɪst]	*n.*	骑自行车的人
cuss	[kʌs]	*vt.*	咒骂
lane	[leɪn]	*n.*	车道
grocery	[ˈɡrəʊsəri]	*n.*	食品杂货店
exorbitant	[ɪɡˈzɔːbɪtənt]	*adj.*	极高的

PHRASES

bring about	带来,导致
air pollution problems	空气污染问题
commit suicide	自杀
global warming	全球变暖

REFERENCE TRANSLATION

生活在汽车时代

人们闭口不谈汽车带来的危险和困难,但对短途旅行自己宁愿开车而不愿骑自行车却有如下辩解:自行车太危险、太不方便。他们自以为开车出行只需为满箱的燃料付费,而把自己花大量时间工作来付购车款及买保险忽略不计。他们要么无视或否认汽车造成的空气污染,要么自以为汽车能使他们远离汽车尾气的危害。(最近研究表明,汽车内部的空气污染远比车外严重。)一位百事通式的人在网上说现在汽车尾气已经干净得不能靠吸入这样的气体来自杀了!他们要么忽视,要么把久坐开车带来的健康问题视为正常,还说骑自行车上班的人有超人的能力。他们极力否认由于人们不愿意改变行为习惯而引起的全球变暖问题的存在。事实上,即使那些承认全球变暖问题的机动车司机也只是在等别人去解决问题。

人们是如何变得这么依赖动力交通的呢？如果我们相信电视或电影中的场景，那么，在拥有汽车之前，似乎每个美国家庭都有一匹马和一辆马车，或者每个人都有自己的马和马鞍。但是，这只是(影视作品)将现有汽车文化向过去时代的投射而已。(在描述美国西部的影片中，马能不进食而飞奔数日。这简直不可思议！)事实上，过去人们每天要花费大量时间来饲养、照顾马匹。因此，大多数人择镇而居，步行就可以到达任何地方。那时，长距离的步行并不稀奇，反而被当作一种享受和乐趣。有人坚持说我们如此依赖汽车是因为我们这个现代化的时代或者是因为我们的富足。然而，世界上其他地区并不像我们这样依赖汽车。在工资和美国一样高的欧洲，每个国家的汽车出行率都不到美国的一半。那些想否认这个事实的人会说："欧洲比美国小，人们都是短途旅行。"除非算上阿拉斯加，否则第一个观点不成立。第二个论断是正确的，因为大体上说，欧洲人无须狂奔50英里去上班。而不管怎样讲，在美国超过半数的出行并未超过5英里。

过去，靠交通工具出行的是富人。即便在没有机动车的朝代，国王尊贵的脚哪怕碰触地面也会被认为不合适。有人为他供膳、沐浴，并有宫女服侍左右。因此，他就成了一个肥胖、无用、不健康甚至会过早夭折的大孩子。显然，这样的目的是尽快地削弱他并尽可能地滋长他的依赖性。同样，在今天的文化中，商家们也竭力使消费者依赖性十足。健康独立的个体能够自己解决问题，对他们来说是无利可图的。我发现我可以仅用30分钟为自己准备一餐美食，其间，我还可以干点别的事情，而整个成本不超过1美元。然而，很多人依赖于加热即食的食品或去餐馆。这些办法成本高，费时多，味道还不好。

但是，人们的交通依赖能产生更大的利润空间。亨利·福特相信，在美国，每个家庭或每个人都将拥有自己的汽车。同时，他极力反对无轨电车的使用，甚至到了不与任何利用无轨电车收发货物的公司有任何商业往来的地步。(事实上，经济大萧条前使用无轨电车运输货物是赚钱的好途径。)无轨电车到底有什么错误？它们不方便吗？它们很昂贵吗？我在拥有无轨电车的城市度过了人生最初的10年。可以这样讲，它们乘坐起来相当有趣，根本不像汽车那样成为麻烦：无轨电车没有后来取代它的公共汽车的污染和噪音。(虽然从那时起，汽车就一直在改进。)的确，我们不得不步行到电车站，但是我们同样可以在目的地直接下车，而不用从停车场再走上一长段路。乘坐电车的费用远低于我们花的停车费。事实上，城市管理者终于意识到，人们把车留在家里会大大降低开销。然而，把汽车留在家中也减少了汽车公司的利润。因为这样一来，汽车就不烧油，也不消耗轮胎。这也就是为什么汽车公司、加油站、汽车轮胎制造商要联手破坏电车线路的真正原因。

今天，当人们说汽车是必需品时，他们实际上是在说我们的社会正竭力使汽车成为必需品。由于人们愿意为节约仅仅5美分而驱车5英里，小型的便利店已在很大程度上萎缩并不断消失。实际上，即使价格并不便宜，很多人也很愿跑这额外的5英里路。以前破旧、弯曲、坡度平缓、行驶缓慢的旧街道被坡度大、车速高的高速路所代替。因为即便是这5英里的路程，人们也已经变得一年比一年更加没有耐心了。年复一年，公路看上去更像竞赛跑道。要想成为一个自行车手是需要鼓足勇气的。

人们坚持说他们喜欢驾车，可我不懂他们从中能享受到什么乐趣。一些司机开车时脏话满嘴：骂自己，也对着路人不耐烦地大喊大叫。我在听到他们之前就能认出这些人。因为他们会违反交通规则，在我离红灯还不到50英尺的时候抢行而差点置我于死地。我父母家旁边有一段三车道的路面。这一路面在进入一段两车道路段之前蜿蜒绕上了一个陡坡。这段陡坡就成了亡命之徒的赛车跑道。那些司机以超过限速10英里的时速盲目地急转弯，就为了第一个冲上山坡。这种开车习惯很容易使我想起在中学课间上完一门课要换教室时所遇到的情形：所有的孩子你推我，我推你，乱作一团。现在马路上也同样乱作一团，而捣乱的就是这同一群人。我猜想如果这帮人真的是想享受驾驶乐趣的话，完全可以慢慢来，大可不必让自己也让别人身处险境。

有人已把奢侈品当作必需品。同这些已经被洗脑的人辩论这个问题是很困难的。改变自己的生活以适应于汽车世界的人坚持认为，离开了汽车，生活是完全不可能的。他们会问："没有车我怎么可以往返100英里去上班？"找一个收入较低一点工作，无须每天奔波100英里，仍然可以过得很惬意。还可以享受很多的空余时间。"那我们怎么送孩子们上学呢？"孩子们自己有腿，不是吗？"要是下雨怎么到校呢？"我步行上学15年，我不曾记得有哪一次雨对我来说是个大问题。"那我们怎么搬运食品杂物或者其他东西呢？"你每天得开着一辆2吨重的车跑来跑去，只是因为你1个月要去一次杂货店买东西？不管怎样，没有汽车并不会挨饿，也不会导致物质匮乏，尽管他们愿意这样认为。事实上，如果不开车而是步行或骑自行车，他们就会发现自己能有更多的余钱在手上，能有更多的闲暇时光，还会有更健康的身体。

如果有人建议我丢掉自行车，我的理由会是什么呢？我说，我不愿错过清晨新鲜的空气、鸟儿的欢唱、充满活力的良好感觉、沿途的鲜花与树木，还有夜晚的星空。为什么有人喜欢把自己封闭在车里开来开去呢？要是我，我会错过很多很好的锻炼机会。因为每周骑上60英里自行车就能达到推荐的适宜运动量。当然，如果花同样的时间步行，效果也是一样的好，尽管这样的步行不能带我去上班或者是去偏远乡村享受愉快的旅行。如果我不得不买车来弥补这一出行上的缺憾的话，我就必须找一份高薪水的工作，住在我不愿意住的地方。

我得承认，并非每个人都能回心转意。即使每个专家都认为地球升温是实实在在的，即使每位医生都告诉他的病人说需要更多的锻炼，即使每条街道都禁止汽车通行，即使所有地方的车速都降到每小时25英里，即使汽油税、停车费及其他的税收项目使得养车的费用过于昂贵，美国人还是会继续热爱并擦亮他们的汽车。像自行车这样普通、实用、方便的交通工具永远也无法赢得他们的青睐。他们在内心会永远热切地渴望那高大的、尾部翘起的、耗油的鲜粉红色1959款凯迪拉克汽车。而且，他们会永远怨恨我们剥夺了他们的乐趣。但是，人们变得成熟而且行为举止有责任心的时代早已一去不复返了。我们这些成熟和具有责任感的人必须和他们错误的想法和做法斗争到底，以改变这个世界的运行模式。否则，我们的子孙后代将无处生存。

Unit 2

Automobile Engines

扫码获取
扩展视频

Fig. 2 - 1 engine

Internal combustion gasoline engines run on a mixture of gasoline and air. The ideal mixture is 14.7 parts of air to one part of gasoline (by weight). Since gas weighs much more than air, we are talking about a whole lot of air and a tiny bit of gas. One part of gas that is completely vaporized into 14.7 parts of air can produce tremendous power when ignited inside an engine.

Air enters the engine through the air cleaner and proceeds to the throttle plate. You control the amount of air that passes through the throttle plate and into the engine with the gas pedal. It is then distributed through a series of passages called the intake manifold, to each cylinder. At some point after the air cleaner, depending on the engine, fuel is added to the air-stream by either a fuel injection system or, in older vehicles, by the carburetor.

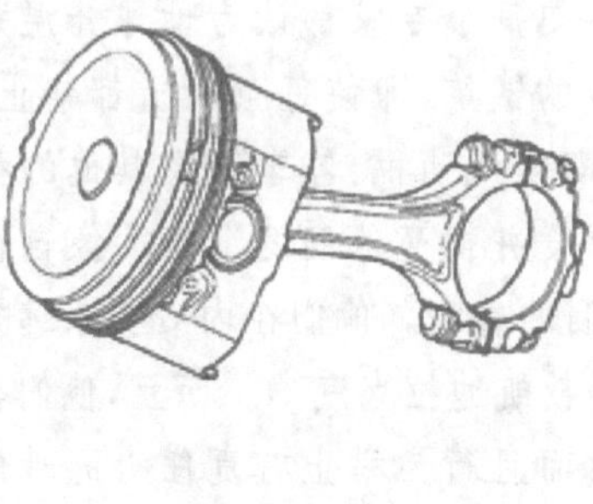

Fig. 2 - 2 typical piston

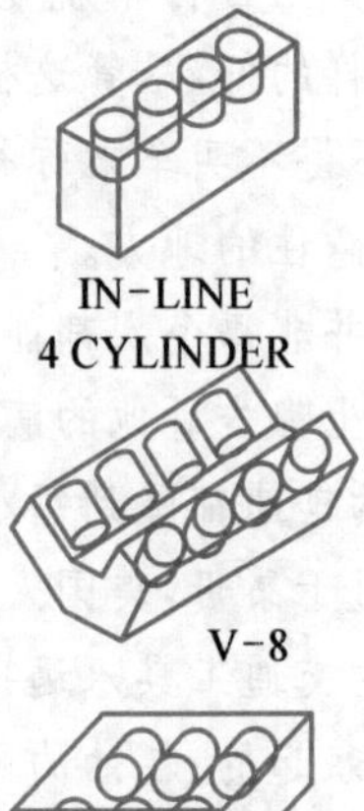

Fig. 2 - 3 cylinder arrangements

Once the fuel is vaporized into the air stream, the mixture is drawn into each cylinder as that cylinder begins its intake stroke. When the piston reaches the bottom of the cylinder, the intake valve closes and the piston begins moving up in the cylinder compressing the charge. When the piston reaches the top, the spark plug ignites the fuel-air mixture causing a powerful expansion of the gas, which pushes the piston back down with great force against the crankshaft, just like a bicycle rider pushing against the pedals to make the bike go.

Engine Types

The majority of engines in motor vehicles today are four-stroke, spark-ignition internal combustion engines. The exceptions like the diesel and rotary engines will not be covered in this article.

There are several engine types which are identified by the number of cylinders and the way the cylinders are laid out. Motor vehicles will have from 3 to 12 cylinders which are arranged in the engine block in several configurations. In-line engines have their cylinders arranged in a row. 3, 4, 5 and 6 cylinder engines commonly use this arrangement. The "V" arrangement uses two banks of cylinders side-by-side and is commonly used in V-6, V-8, V-10 and V-12 configurations. Flat engines use two opposing banks of cylinders and are less common than the other two designs. They are used in engines from Subaru and Porsche in 4 and 6 cylinder arrangements as well as in the old VW beetles with 4 cylinders. Flat engines are also used in some Ferraris with 12 cylinders.

Most engine blocks are made of cast iron or cast aluminum. Each cylinder contains a piston that travels up and down inside the cylinder bore. All the pistons in the engine are connected through individual connecting rods to a common cankshaft.

Fig. 2-4 crankshaft

The crankshaft is located below the cylinders on an in-line engine, at the base of the V on a V-type engine and between the cylinder banks on a flat engine. As the pistons move up and down, they turn the crankshaft just like your legs pump up and down to turn the crank that is connected to the pedals of a bicycle.

A cylinder head is bolted to the top of each bank of cylinders to seal the individual cylinders and contain the combustion process that takes place inside the cylinder. Most cylinder heads are made of cast aluminum or cast iron. The cylinder head contains at least one intake valve and one exhaust valve for each cylinder. This allows the air-fuel mixture to enter the cylinder and the burned exhaust gas to exit the cylinder. Many newer engines are using multiple intake and exhaust valves per cylinder for increased engine power and efficiency.

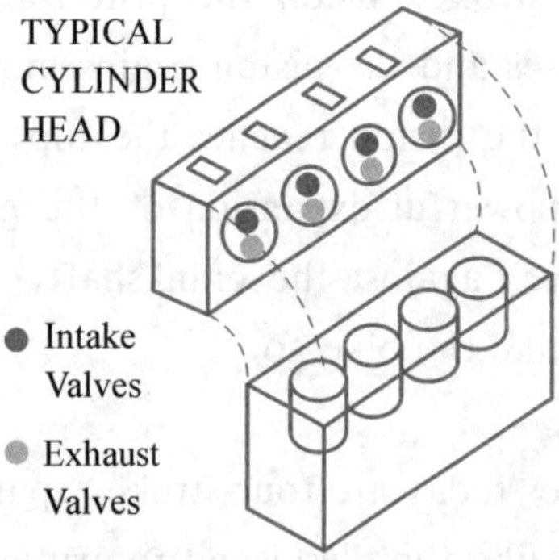

Fig. 2-5　cylinder head

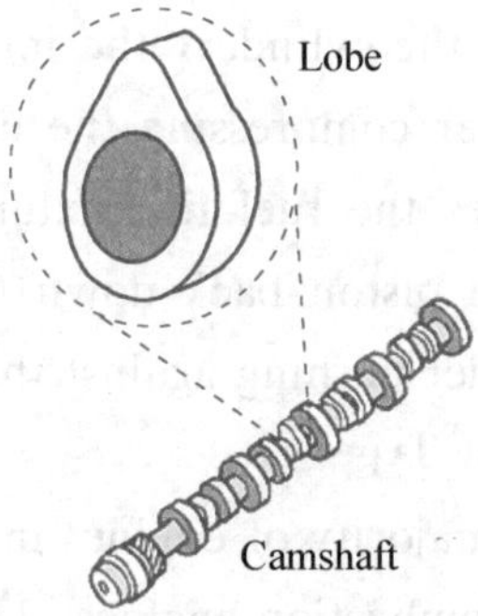

Fig. 2-6　camshaft

The valves are opened and closed by means of a camshaft. A camshaft is a rotating shaft that has individual lobes for each valve. The lobe is a "bump" on one side of the shaft that pushes against a valve lifter moving it up and down. When the lobe pushes against the lifter, the lifter in turn pushes the valve open. When the lobe rotates away from the lifter, the valve is closed by a spring that is attached to the valve. A common configuration is to have one camshaft located in the engine block with the lifters connecting to the valves through a series of linkages. The camshaft must be synchronized with the crankshaft so that the camshaft makes one revolution for every two revolutions of the crankshaft. In most engines, this is done by a "Timing Chain" (similar to a bicycle chain) that connects the camshaft with the crankshaft. Newer engines have the camshaft located in the cylinder head directly over the valves. This design is more efficient but it is more costly to manufacture and requires multiple camshafts on Flat and V-type engines. It also requires much longer timing chains or timing belts which are prone to wear. Some engines have two camshafts on each head, one for the intake valves and one for the exhaust valves. These engines are called Double Overhead Camshaft (D.O.H.C.) Engines while the other type is called Single Overhead.

How an Engine Works

Since the same process occurs in each cylinder, we will take a look at one cylinder to see how the four stroke process works. The four strokes are Intake, Compression, Power and Exhaust. The piston travels down on the Intake stroke, up on the Compression stroke, down on the Power stroke and up on the Exhaust stroke.

Intake

As the piston starts down on the Intake stroke, the intake valve opens and the fuel-air mixture is drawn into the cylinder (similar to drawing back the plunger on a hypodermic needle to allow fluid to be drawn into the chamber). When the piston reaches the bottom of the intake stroke, the intake valve closes, trapping the air-fuel mixture in the cylinder.

Compression

The piston moves up and compresses the trapped air fuel mixture that was brought in by the intake stroke. The amount of the mixture compressed is determined by the compression ratio of the engine. The compression ratio on the average engine is in the range of 8 : 1 to 10 : 1. This means that when the piston reaches the top of the cylinder, the air-fuel mixture is squeezed to about one tenth of its original volume.

Power

The spark plug fires, igniting the compressed air-fuel mixture which produces a powerful expansion of the vapor. The combustion process pushes the piston down the cylinder with great force turning the crankshaft to provide the power to propel the vehicle. Each piston fires at a different time, determined by the engine firing order. By the time the crankshaft completes two revolutions, each cylinder in the engine will have gone through one power stroke.

Exhaust

With the piston at the bottom of the cylinder, the exhaust valve opens to allow the burned exhaust gas to be expelled to the exhaust system. Since the cylinder contains so much pressure, when the valve opens, the gas is expelled with a violent force (that is why a vehicle without a muffler sounds so loud). The piston travels up to the top of the cylinder pushing all the exhaust out before closing the exhaust valve in preparation for starting the four stroke process over again.

Engine Balance

To keep the combustion pulses from generating a vibration, a flywheel is attached to the back of the crankshaft. The flywheel is a disk that is about 12 to 15 inches in diameter. On a standard transmission car, the flywheel is a heavy iron disk that doubles as part of the clutch system. On automatic equipped vehicles, the flywheel is a stamped steel plate that mounts the heavy torque converter. The flywheel uses inertia to smooth out the normal engine pulses.

NEW WORDS

vaporize	[ˈveɪpəraɪz]	*v.*	汽化
throttle	[ˈθrɔtl]	*n.*	节气门
injection	[inˈdʒekʃn]	*n.*	喷射

diesel	[ˈdiːzl]	*n*.	柴油机
block	[blɒk]	*n*.	缸体
seal	[siːl]	*n*.	密封
camshaft	[ˈkæmʃɑːft]	*n*.	凸轮轴
synchronize	[ˈsɪŋkrənaɪz]	*v*.	使同步
overhead	[ˈəuvəhed]	*adj*.	顶置的
intake	[ˈɪnteɪk]	*n*.	进气
flywheel	[ˈflaɪwiːl]	*n*.	飞轮
disk	[dɪsk]	*adj*.	盘式的
vibration	[vaɪˈbreiʃn]	*n*.	振动
pump	[pʌmp]	*n*.	泵
mixture	[ˈmɪkstʃə]	*n*.	混合气
pedal	[ˈpedl]	*n*.	踏板
cylinder	[ˈsɪlɪndə]	*n*.	缸套
crankshaft	[ˈkræŋkʃɑːft]	*n*.	曲轴
stroke	[strəuk]	*n*.	冲程

PHRASES

intake stroke	吸气冲程
compression stroke	压缩冲程
power stroke	做功冲程
exhaust stroke	排气冲程
torque convertor	液力变矩器
spark plug	火花塞

REVIEW QUESTIONS

(1) What does "DOHC 24 Valve V6" mean?
(2) List the engine type you know.
(3) What is the function of the cylinder head?
(4) Show the whole work process of engines.
(5) Why do new models use the multiply-valve technology?
(6) Tell us two ways to prevent an engine from over vibration.

REFERENCE TRANSLATION

汽车发动机

内燃汽油发动机依靠空燃混合气工作，理想混合气空燃比以重量计为14.7比1，因汽油比空气重很多，所以混合气是大量的空气和一小部分汽油，一份汽油完全挥发在14.7份空气中在发动机里点燃时会产生巨大的能量。

空气经空滤器和节气门进入发动机，用油门踏板控制通过节气门进入发动机的空气量，然后经称为进气歧管的一系列气道分配到每个气缸，根据机型不同，在空滤后的某个位置，汽油由燃油喷射系统而在老式汽车中由化油器添加到空气流中。

一旦汽油挥发进入空气流，混合气吸入气缸，气缸开始进气冲程，当活塞进入气缸底部，进气门关闭，活塞开始在气缸内上行压缩混合气，当活塞到达顶部，火花塞点燃混合气引起空气急剧膨胀，克服曲轴阻力强力推动活塞下行。如同骑手踩动踏板使自行车前行一样。

发动机类型

现在大多数汽车发动机都是四冲程火花塞点燃式内燃机，例外的如柴油机和旋转式发动机本文不讨论。

发动机分类通过缸数与布置形式区分，汽车一般有三到十二缸以几种形式排列在缸体上。直列式气缸一字型排列，3，4，5，6缸多为这种形式，V型发动机气缸并肩排在缸体两边，常见是有V6，V8，V10和V12，斯巴鲁和保时捷四六缸、老款大众甲壳虫四缸采用水平对置式，发动机两组气缸相对而置，比前两种使用少很多，12缸法拉利也是这种发动机。

大多缸体由铸铁或铸铝制成，每个缸有一个活塞在缸内壁上下运行，发动机所有活塞通过各自连杆与同一曲轴相连。

曲轴位于直列式发动机底部，V型中线，水平对置式中间，随着活塞上下运行，推动曲轴转动，如同你的腿踩自行车踏板带动曲拐一样。

缸头用螺栓连接在气缸顶部起密封作用，缸头多由铸铁或铝制成，缸头上每个缸至少有一个进气门一个排气门，使空燃混合气可以进入气缸，烧完的尾气排出气缸，许多新型发动机采用每缸多气门以增加发动机动力和效率。

气门开关由凸轮轴控制，凸轮轴是旋转轴，每个气门对应一个凸轮，凸轮是轴一边的凸起推动气门推杆上下运动，当凸起推动推杆时气门打开，当凸起远离推杆时，气门由弹簧复位而关闭。常见形式是凸轮轴位于缸体下部，以推杆与连杆件与气门相连，凸轮轴需与曲轴协同工作，曲轴转二圈凸轮轴转一圈，大多数发动机通过“正时链”(类似于自行车链条)将两者相连，这种形式效率较高但在V型和水平对置发动机上制造成本较高，且链条较长，而正时带易于磨损。有些发动机缸头上有两个凸轮轴，分别用于进排气门控制，这种发动机叫双顶置凸轮轴，否则叫单顶置凸轮轴。

发动机工作原理

因每个缸工作过程相同，我们可以通过一个缸了解四冲程的工作过程，四冲程是进气、压缩、做功和排气。进气时活塞下行，上行压缩，下行做功，上行排气。

进气

进气冲程时活塞开始下行，进气门打开，空燃混合气吸入气缸，(类似于注射针管柱塞回拉吸入注射液)。活塞到达进气行程底部时，进气门关闭，空燃混合气被封入气缸。

压缩

活塞上行压缩由进气行程吸入的密封的混合气，混合气的压缩量取决于发动机压缩比，一般压缩比在八至十比一之间，意思是活塞上行到气缸顶部时，混合气被压成原体积的十分之一左右。

做功

火花塞点火，点燃压缩气产生气体的急剧膨胀，燃烧过程推动活塞沿气缸下行，带着巨大的推力推动曲轴产生动力驱动汽车，每个缸点火时间不同，由发动机点火顺序决定，曲轴转两圈，发动机每个缸做一次功。

排气

活塞位于气缸底部时，排气门打开，让燃烧完的尾气排出排气系统，因缸压很大，排气门打开时，尾气具有很大的冲力(这就是为什么不装消音器时噪声很大)。活塞上行到气缸顶部，在排气门关闭前排出所有尾气，为下一次四冲程做好准备。

发动机动平衡

为防止燃烧脉冲产生发动机振动，在曲轴后部安装飞轮，飞轮是个直径约 12 到 15 英寸圆盘，在手动变速器汽车上，飞轮是个较重的铸铁盘，也是离合器的一部件，在自动变速器汽车上，飞轮是个锻钢盘安装在液力变矩器上。飞轮利用惯性来吸收发动机振动。

Unit 3

Car Steering System

扫码获取
扩展视频

The direction of the automobile under way is changed by turning the front wheels with the aid of the steering system. The steering system includes a steering gear and a steering control linkage. The rotation of the steering wheel is imparted to the levers and rods of the linkage by which the steerable wheels are turned.

Turning the Car

For a car to turn smoothly, each wheel must follow a different circle. Since the inside wheel is following a circle with a smaller radius, it is actually making a tighter turn than the outside wheel. If you draw a line perpendicular to each wheel, the lines will intersect at the center point of the turn. The geometry of the steering linkage makes the inside wheel turn more than the outside wheel.

There are a couple different types of steering gears. The most common are rack-and-pinion and recirculating ball.

Rack-and-Pinion Steering

Rack-and-pinion steering is quickly becoming the most common type of steering on cars, small trucks and SUVs. It is actually a pretty simple mechanism. A rack-and-pinion gearset is enclosed in a metal tube, with each end of the rack protruding from the tube. A rod, called a tie rod, connects to each end of the rack. The pinion gear is attached to the steering shaft. When you turn the steering wheel, the gear spins, moving the rack. The tie rod at each end of the rack connects to the steering arm on the spindle.

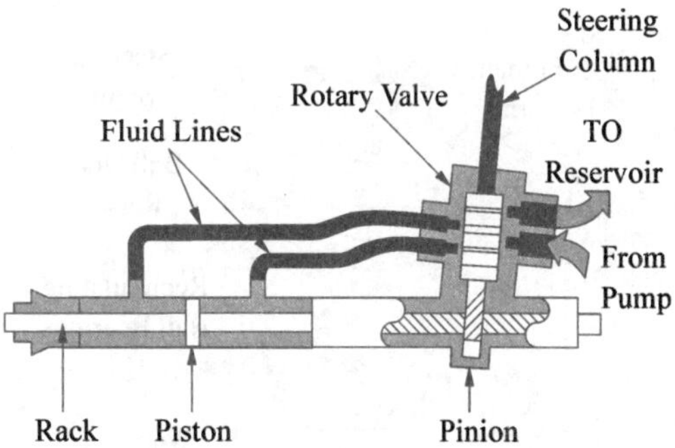

Fig. 3-1 power steering system

The Rack-and-Pinion Gearset Does Two Things:

It converts the rotational motion of the steering wheel into the linear motion needed to turn the wheels.

It provides a gear reduction, making it easier to turn the wheels.

On most cars, it takes three to four complete revolutions of the steering wheel to make the wheels turn from lock to lock (from far left to far right).

The steering ratio is the ratio of how far you turn the steering wheel to how far the wheels turn. For instance, if one complete revolution (360 degrees) of the steering wheel results in the wheels of the car turning 20 degrees, then the steering ratio is 360 divided by 20, or 18 : 1. A higher ratio means that you have to turn the steering wheel more to get the wheels to turn a given distance. However, less effort is required because of the higher gear ratio.

Generally, lighter, sportier cars have lower steering ratios than larger cars and trucks. The lower ratio gives the steering a quicker response—you don't have to turn the steering wheel as much to get the wheels to turn a given distance—which is a desirable trait in sports cars. These smaller cars are light enough that even with the lower ratio, the effort required to turn the steering wheel is not excessive.

Some cars have variable-ratio steering, which uses a rack-and-pinion gearset that has a different tooth pitch (number of teeth per inch) in the center than it has on the outside. This makes the car respond quickly when starting a turn (the rack is near the center), and also reduces effort near the wheel's turning limits.

Power Rack-and-Pinion

When the rack-and-pinion is in a power-steering system, the rack has a slightly different design.

Part of the rack contains a cylinder with a piston in the middle. The piston is connected to the rack. There are two fluid ports, one on either side of the piston. Supplying higher-pressure fluid to one side of the piston forces the piston to move, which in turn moves the rack, providing the power assist.

We'll check out the components that provide the high-pressure fluid, as well as decide which side of the rack to supply it to, later in the article. First, let's take a look at another type of steering.

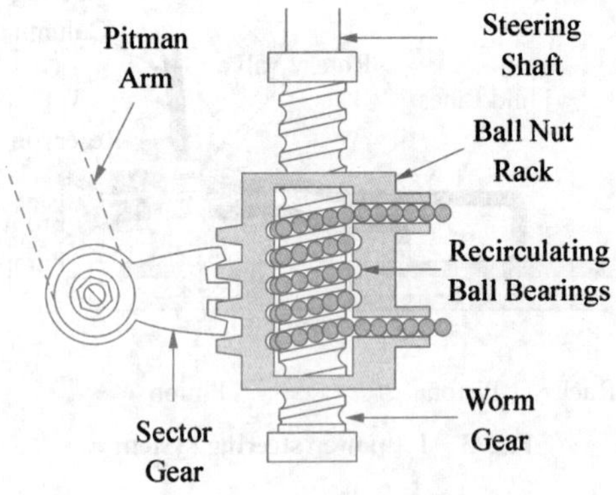

Fig. 3 - 2 recirculating ball steering gear

Recirculating-Ball Steering

Recirculating-ball steering is used on many trucks and SUVs today. The linkage that turns the wheels is slightly different than on a rack-and-pinion system. The recirculating-ball steering gear contains a worm gear. You can image the gear in two parts. The first part is a block of metal with a threaded hole in it. This block has gear teeth cut into the outside of it, which engage a gear that moves the pitman arm. The steering wheel connects to a threaded rod, similar to a bolt. When the steering wheel turns, it turns the bolt. Instead of twisting further into the block the way a regular bolt would, this bolt is held fixed so that when it spins, it moves the block, which moves the gear that turns the wheels.

Instead of the bolt directly engaging the threads in the block, all of the threads are filled with ball bearings that recirculate through the gear as it turns. The balls actually serve two purposes: First, they reduce friction and wear in the gear; second, they reduce slop in the gear. Slop would be felt when you change the direction of the steering wheel—without the balls in the steering gear, the teeth would come out of contact with each other for a moment, making the steering wheel feel loose.

Power steering in a recirculating-ball system works similarly to a rack-and-pinion system. Assist is provided by supplying higher-pressure fluid to one side of the block.

Now let's take a look at the other components that make up a power-steering system.

Power Steering

There are a couple of key components in power steering in addition to the rack-and-pinion or recirculating-ball mechanism.

Pump

The hydraulic power for the steering is provided by a rotary-vane pump.This pump is driven by the car's engine via a belt and pulley.

As the vanes spin, they pull hydraulic fluid from the return line at low pressure and force it into the outlet at high pressure. The amount of flow provided by the pump depends on the car's engine speed. The pump must be designed to provide adequate flow when the engine is idling.

The pump contains a pressure-relief valve to make sure that the pressure does not get too high.

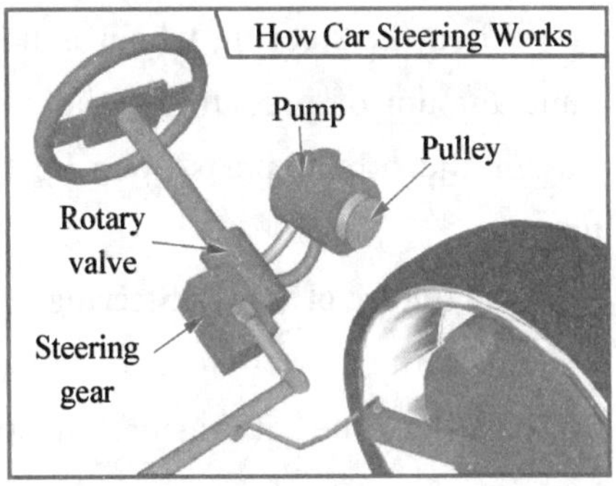

Fig. 3 - 3 hydraulic power steering system

Rotary Valve

A power-steering system should assist the driver only when he is exerting force on the steering wheel (such as when starting a turn). When the driver is not exerting force (such as when driving in a straight line), the system shouldn't provide any assist. The device that senses the force on the steering wheel is called the rotary valve.

The input from the steering shaft forms the inner part of a spool-valve assembly. It also connects to the top end of the torsion bar. The bottom of the torsion bar connects to the outer part of the spool valve. The torsion bar also turns the output of the steering gear, connecting to either the pinion gear or the worm gear depending on which type of steering the car has.

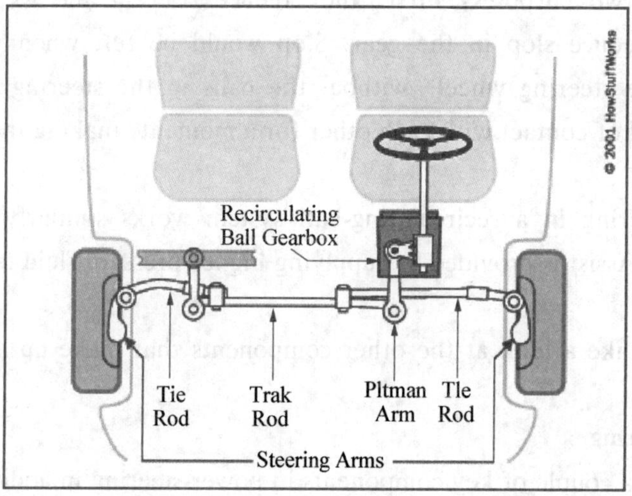

Fig. 3 - 4 steering system

As the bar twists, it rotates the inside of the spool valve relative to the outside. The amount of rotation between the inner and outer parts of the spool valve depends on how much torque the driver applies to the steering wheel.

When the steering wheel is not being turned, both hydraulic lines provide the same amount of pressure to the steering gear. But if the spool valve is turned one way or the other, ports open up to provide high-pressure fluid to the appropriate line.

The Future of Power Steering

Since the power-steering pump on most cars today runs constantly, pumping fluid all the time, it wastes horsepower. This wasted power translates into wasted fuel.

One of the coolest ideas is the "steer-by-wire" or "drive-by-wire" system. These systems would completely eliminate the mechanical connection between the steering wheel and the steering, replacing it with a purely electronic control system. It would contain sensors that tell the car what the driver is doing with the wheel, and have some motors in it to provide the driver with feedback on what the car is doing. The output of these sensors would be used to control a motorized steering system. This would free up space in the engine compartment by eliminating the steering shaft. It would also reduce vibration inside the car.

General Motors has introduced a concept car, the Hy-wire, that features this type of driving system. One of the most exciting things about the drive-by-wire system in the GM Hy-wire is that you can fine-tune vehicle handling without changing anything in the car's mechanical components—all it takes to adjust the steering is some new computer software.

NEW WORDS

impart	[ɪm'pɑːt]	*v.*	通知，传给
radius	['reɪdiəs]	*n.*	半径
perpendicular	[ˌpɜːpən'dɪkjələ]	*adj.*	垂直的
retractable	[rɪ'træktəbl]	*adj.*	可收回的
intersect	[ˌɪntə'sekt]	*v.*	交叉
geometry	[dʒi'ɒmətri]	*n.*	几何学
protrude	[prə'truːd]	*v.*	突出
spindle	['spɪndl]	*n.*	轴
effort	['efət]	*n.*	力
trait	[treɪt]	*n.*	特性
pitch	[pɪtʃ]	*n.*	节距
thread	[θred]	*n.*	螺纹
bolt	[bəult]	*v.*	用螺栓连接
friction	['frɪkʃn]	*n.*	摩擦
via	['viːə]	*v.*	经过
vane	[veɪn]	*n.*	叶片
exert	[ɪg'zɜːt]	*v.*	施加
torque	[tɔːk]	*n.*	力矩
spool	[spuːl]	*adj.*	转动的
eliminate	[ɪ'lɪmɪneɪt]	*v.*	消除

PHRASES

steering gear	方向机

recirculating ball	循环球式
rack-and-pinion	齿轮齿条式
steering ratio	方向盘转角比
rotary-vane pump	叶片泵
pressure-relief valve	减压阀
spool-valve	随动阀

REVIEW QUESTIONS

(1) What's the function of the rack-and-pinion gearset?

(2) What's the meaning of the "steering ratio"?

(3) Please introduce the "variable-ratio steering".

(4) How does the power rack-and-pinion work?

(5) what is function of the balls in the recirculating-ball steering system?

REFERENCE TRANSLATION

汽车转向系统

行驶中汽车的方向通过借助于转向系统转动前轮实现转向，转向系统包括方向机和连接件，方向盘的转动传给连杆，再转动转向轮。

转向

汽车要转向平稳，每个车轮需转向半径不同，因内侧轮转弯半径较小，实际上就是比外侧车轮转向要急，如对每个车轮正交画线，四根线会交于一点，转向连杆的几何性质决定内侧比外侧车轮转向角大。

方向机有多种类型，最常见的是齿轮齿条式和循环球式。

齿轮齿条式转向

齿轮齿条式转向很快就成为轿车、轻卡和SUV最常见的方向机，实际上机械结构相当简单，齿轮齿条式方向机封装于金属管中，两端突出连接连杆，小齿轮安装在方向柱上。转动方向盘时，小齿轮旋转推动齿条，两端的连杆带动方向臂上转动。

齿轮齿条式方向机的两个作用

第一个作用是将方向盘的旋转运动转变为转动车轮所需要的直线运动。

第二个作用是产生传动比，使转向较轻便。

大多数汽车，方向盘转三四圈对应车轮最大转角(最左和最右的角度)。

传动比指转动方向盘的距离与车轮转动的角度之比。如方向盘转一整圈(360度)车轮转20度，传动比是360除以20即18∶1，传动比在意味着车轮转相同距离方向盘转动的角度需大一些，但由于传动比作用需要的力量较小。

一般地，轻型、运动型车比大型车、卡车的传动比小，传动比小，转向轮反应快，车轮转角相同时打方向盘的角度不需要那么大，这是运动型车所需要的优点，这些小型车重量足够轻，即使传动比较小，施加到方向盘的力也不是太大。

有些车传动比可变，其齿轮齿条的螺距（每英寸长所有的齿数）中间与外侧不一样，这样，汽车开始转向时反应快捷（齿条位于中心），转向接近左右死角时需要的力量较小。

助力齿轮齿条式

动力转向系统中的齿轮齿条式方向机，齿条结构稍有不同。

齿条的一部分有一油缸，中间装有活塞与齿条相边连，活塞两端各有一油口，活塞一侧供给高压油推动活塞运动，即推动齿条产生助力转向。

在本文后面，我们会讨论产生高压油的部件和哪一侧供高压油。先让我看下另一种循环球式方向机。

循环球式转向

现在许多卡车和SUV使用循环球式，其与转向轮的连接与齿轮齿条式稍有不同。循环球式有一个螺母，你可以将其想象为两个部分，第一部分是具有螺纹孔的金属柱，柱的外侧切成齿形，其与一只齿轮结合驱动转向臂，方向盘连在螺纹杆（类似螺栓）上，方向盘转动时，螺栓旋转，与普通螺栓不同，不是越转越远，螺杆固定住不能上下移动，这样，其转动时，螺母上下移动带动齿轮转动车轮。

螺杆不是直接与螺母相接触，而在螺纹中充满球轴承，方向盘转动时，球在其中循环，实际上起两个作用：第一是减少摩擦和齿轮磨损，第二是减少游隙，在改变方向盘方向时会感觉得到自由行程，如没球在里面，齿轮会有一会不能相互接触，使方向盘感觉松旷。

动力转向的循环球与齿轮齿条式相似，高压油输入到一侧产生助力作用。

现在看下动力转向的一些部件构成。

动力转向

除齿轮齿条和循环球外，动力转向中还有一些主要部件。

泵

旋转叶片泵提供转向液压动力，经皮带与带轮由发动机提供动力。

叶片旋转带动来自回油管的低压油从高压出口流出，泵的流量取决于发动机速度，泵需设计成在怠速时可提供足够的流量。油泵有一个泄压阀保证压力不至于太高。

转阀

动向转向系统应该是只在驾驶员打方向盘（如开始转向）时起助力作用，而驾驶员不施力（如直行）时，系统不会起助力作用，表征有否给方向盘施力的装置是转阀。

转向柱传给随动阀内部元件，它也与扭力杆顶端相连，扭力杆底部与转阀外部元件相接，扭力杆也转向方向机的输出，连接到小齿轮或蜗轮，取决于转向车的类型。

随着扭力杆扭转，它转动阀芯的内部（相对于外部）。该滑阀的内侧和外侧部分之间的旋转量的多少取决于驾驶员施加到方向盘的转矩大小。

当转向轮不转，两条液压管路提供相同压力给方向机。但如果阀芯只向任意一侧转动，出油口开放向对应的管线提供高压油。

动力转向的未来

因动力转向泵在现在大多数车上都是连续运转，不断供油，浪费功率等于是浪费燃油。

最酷的想法是“电控”或“电驱动”系统。这些系统将完全消除转向盘和转向之间的机械连接，取而代之的是一个纯粹的电子控制系统。它将包含传感器，告诉汽车现在司机在如何操作方向盘，有些汽车还会提供驾驶员汽车工作状态反馈信号，这些传感器的输出可用于电动转向系统的控制。通过消除转向轴将在引擎室腾出空间，它也会降低车内振动。

通用汽车研制了一种概念车，HY－WIRE是其驱动系统的一个亮点，现有电子控制转向系统最令人激动的是GM的HY－WIRE系统，可以不需要改变任何机械元件地调整汽车转向，只需用计算机软件即可进行转向系统的调整。

Unit 4

Four-Wheel Drive

扫码获取
扩展视频

There are almost as many different types of four-wheel-drive systems as there are four-wheel-drive vehicles. It seems that every manufacturer has several different schemes for providing power to all of the wheels. The language used by the different carmakers can sometimes be a little confusing, so before we get started explaining how they work, let's clear up some terminology:

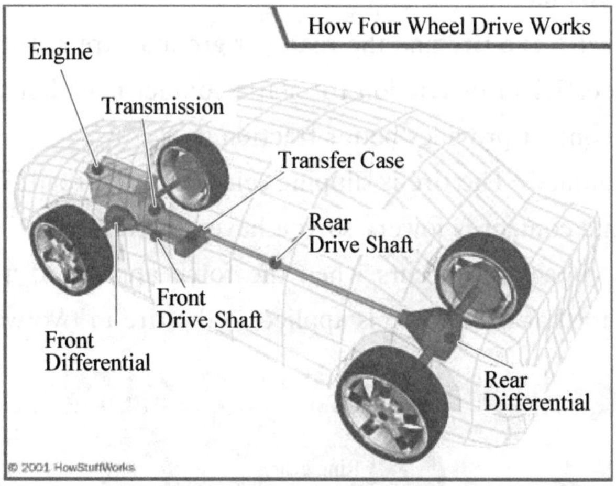

Fig. 4 - 1 four-wheel-drive

Four-wheel drive—Usually, when carmakers say that a car has four-wheel drive, they are referring to a part-time system. These systems are meant only for use in low-traction conditions, such as off-road or on snow or ice.

All-wheel drive—These systems are sometimes called full-time four-wheel drive. All-wheel-drive systems are designed to function on all types of surfaces, both on- and off-road, and most of them cannot be switched off.

Torque, Traction and Wheel Slip

Torque is the twisting force that the engine produces. The torque from the engine is what moves your car. More torque can be sent to the wheels in first gear than in fifth gear because first gear has a larger gear-ratio by which to multiply the torque. The interesting thing about torque is that in low-traction situations, the maximum amount of torque that can be created is determined by the amount of traction, not by the engine.

We'll define traction as the maximum amount of force the tire can apply against the ground (or that the ground can apply against the tire—they're the same thing). These are the factors that affect traction:

1. The weight on the tire—The more weight on a tire, the more traction it has. Weight can shift as a car drives. For instance, when a car makes a turn, weight shifts to the outside wheels. When it accelerates, weight shifts to the rear wheels.

2. The coefficient of friction—This factor relates the amount of friction force between two surfaces to the force holding the two surfaces together. In our case, it relates the amount of traction between the tires and the road to the weight resting on each tire.

3. Wheel slip—There are two kinds of contact that tires can make with the road: static and dynamic.

4. Static contact—The tire and the road (or ground) are not slipping relative to each other. The coefficient of friction for static contact is higher than for dynamic contact, so static contact provides better traction.

5. Dynamic contact—The tire is slipping relative to the road. The coefficient of friction for dynamic contact is lower, so you have less traction.

Quite simply, wheel slip occurs when the force applied to a tire exceeds the traction available to that tire. Force is applied to the tire in two ways:

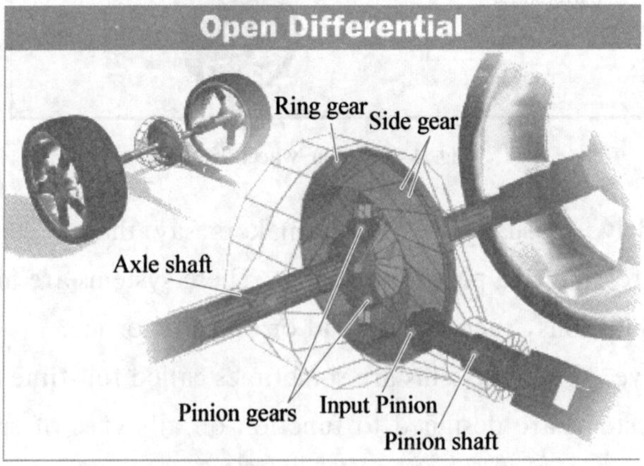

Fig. 4 - 2 the open differential

Longitudinally—Longitudinal force comes from the torque applied to the tire by the engine or by the brakes. It tends to either accelerate or decelerate the car.

Laterally—Lateral force is created when the car drives around a curve. It takes force to make a car change direction—ultimately, the tires and the ground provide lateral force.

Most people don't even come close to exceeding the available traction on dry pavement, or even on flat, wet pavement. Four-wheel and all-wheel-drive systems are most useful in low-traction situations, such as in snow and on slippery hills.

Four-wheel drive can help in a variety of situations. For instance:

In snow—It takes a lot of force to push a car through the snow. The amount of force available is limited by the available traction. Most two-wheel-drive cars can't move if there is more than a few inches of snow on the road, because in the snow, each tire has only a small amount of traction. A four-wheel-drive car can utilize the traction of all four tires.

Off road—In off-road conditions, it is fairly common for at least one set of tires to be in a low-traction situation, such as when crossing a stream or mud puddle. With four-wheel drive, the other set of tires still has traction, so they can pull you out.

Climbing slippery hills—This task requires a lot of traction. A four-wheel-drive car can utilize the traction of all four tires to pull the car up the hill.

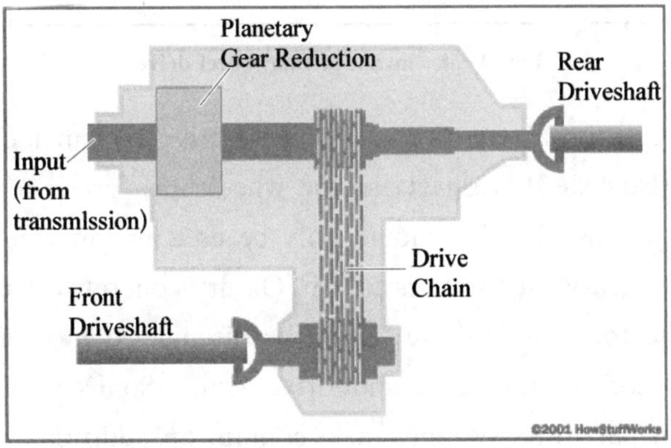

Fig. 4 - 3 part time four-wheel drive transfer case

There are also some situations in which four-wheel drive provides no advantage over two-wheel drive. Most notably, four-wheel-drive systems won't help you stop on slippery surfaces. It's all up to the brakes and the anti-lock braking system (ABS).

Components of a Four-Wheel-Drive System

The main parts of any four-wheel-drive system are the two differentials (front and rear) and the transfer case. In addition, part-time systems have locking hubs, and both types of systems may have advanced electronics that help them make even better use of the available traction.

Differentials: A car has two differentials, one located between the two front wheels and one between the two rear wheels. They send the torque from the driveshaft or transmission to the drive wheels. They also allow the left and right wheels to spin at different speeds when you go around a turn.

Transfer Case

This is the device that splits the power between the front and rear axles on a four-wheel-drive car.

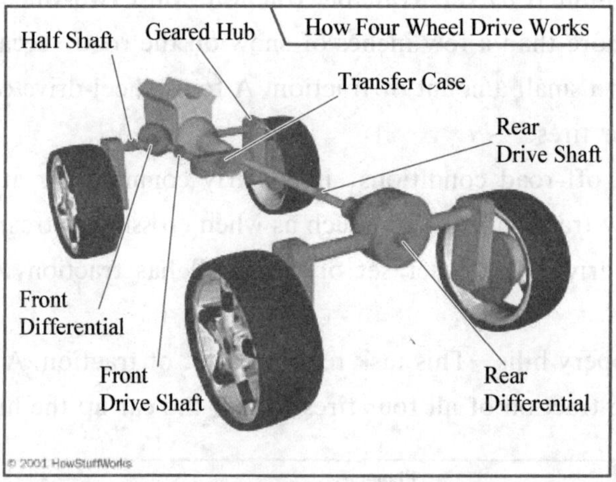

Fig. 4 - 4　layout of four wheel drive

The transfer case on a part-time four-wheel-drive system locks the front-axle driveshaft to the rear-axle driveshaft, so the wheels are forced to spin at the same speed. Part-time systems like this should only be used in low-traction situations in which it is relatively easy for the tires to slip. On dry concrete, it is not easy for the tires to slip, so the four-wheel drive should be disengaged in order to avoid jerky turns and extra wear on the tires and drive train. Some transfer cases, more commonly those in part-time systems, also contain an additional set of gears that give the vehicle a low range. This extra gear ratio gives the vehicle extra torque and a super-slow output speed. In first gear in low range, the vehicle might have a top speed of about 5 mph (8 kph), but incredible torque is produced at the wheels. This allows drivers to slowly and smoothly creep up very steep hills.

Locking Hubs

Each wheel in a car is bolted to a hub. Part-time four-wheel-drive trucks usually have locking hubs on the front wheels. When four-wheel drive is not engaged, the locking hubs are used to disconnect the front wheels from the front differential, half-shafts (the shafts that connect the differential to the hub) and driveshaft. This allows the differential, half-shafts and driveshaft to stop spinning when the car is in two-wheel drive, saving wear and tear on those parts and improving fuel-economy.

Advanced Electronics

On many modern four-wheel and all-wheel-drive vehicles, advanced electronics play a key role. Some cars use the ABS system to selectively apply the brakes to wheels that start to skid—this is called brake-traction control. Others have sophisticated, electronically-controlled clutches that can better control the torque transfer between wheels.

A Basic System

The type of part-time system typically found on four-wheel-drive pickups and older SUVs works like this: The vehicle is usually rear-wheel drive. The transmission hooks up directly to a transfer case. From there, one driveshaft turns the front axle, and another turns the rear axle.

When four-wheel drive is engaged, the transfer case locks the front driveshaft to the rear driveshaft, so each axle receives half of the torque coming from the engine. At the same time, the front hubs lock.

Previously, we said that the best four-wheel-drive system will send exactly the right amount of torque to each wheel, the right amount being the maximum torque that won't cause that tire to slip. This system rates fairly poorly by that criterion. It sends to both wheels the amount of torque that won't cause the tire with the least traction to slip.

NEW WORDS

scheme	[skiːm]	*n.* & *v.*	技术,方案
traction	[ˈtrækʃn]	*n.*	牵引力
coefficient	[ˌkəuɪˈfɪʃnt]	*n.*	系数
longitudinally	[ˌlɔndʒɪˈtjuːdɪnəlɪ]	*adv.*	纵向地
pavement	[ˈpeɪvmənt]	*n.*	公路
axle	[æksl]	*n.*	轮轴, 车轴
confuse	[kənˈfjuːz]	*v.*	使糊涂
terminology	[ˌtɜːmɪˈnɒlədʒi]	*n.*	术语
decelerate	[diːˈseləreɪt]	*v.*	减速
lateral	[ˈlætərəl]	*a.*	侧向的
criterion	[kraɪˈtɪəriən]	*n.*	标准
slippery	[ˈslɪpəri]	*adj.*	滑的

PHRASES

four-wheel-drive 四轮驱动
the coefficient of friction 摩擦系数
part-time FWD 分时四轮驱动
full time FWD 全时四轮驱动

REVIEW QUESTIONS

(1) What is the difference between the four-wheel drive and all-wheel drive?
(2) More torque can be sent to the wheels in first gear than in fifth gear, why?
(3) List the factors that affect traction.
(4) What is the right amount torque for driving system?
(5) Why do cars used in cities seldom use the four wheel drive system?

REFERENCE TRANSLATION

四轮驱动系统

几乎有多少四轮驱动的车辆就有多少类型的四轮驱动系统。似乎，每个制造商都有几种提供车轮动力的方案。因不同的制造商使用的术语是有差异的，所以在我们开始解释它们的工作原理之前，让我们澄清一些术语：

四轮驱动——通常，当汽车制造商说，一辆汽车有四驱，他们指的是分时四驱。这些系统只在低牵引力条件下使用，如越野、雪地或冰面。

全轮驱动——这些系统有时被称为全时四驱。全轮驱动系统用于所有类型的路况，无论是公路还是越野，他们中的大多数无法切换成两驱。

扭矩、牵引力和车轮滑移

转矩是指发动机产生的扭转力矩。正是发动机扭矩驱动你的汽车。第一挡比五挡传给车轮的扭矩多，因为第一挡具有较大的传动比，扭矩得以增加。有趣的是，在低附着力的情况下最大扭矩取决于牵引力而不是发动机。

我们将牵引力定义为轮胎施加给地面的最大量的力（或地面给轮胎的力——它们是同一件事）。以下都是牵引力的影响因素。

1. 轮胎承重：轮胎承重越大，牵引力越大。汽车行驶时，承重会偏移，例如，当汽车转弯时，重量转移到外侧车轮。它加速时，重量转移到后轮。

2. 摩擦系数：系数大小与保持两表面相互接触摩擦力相关。在此，与轮胎和路面的摩擦力相关,也与每个轮胎的承重有关。

3. 车轮滑移:轮胎与道路间有两种接触方式:静摩擦和动摩擦。

4. 静摩擦:轮胎与路面(或地面)无相对滑动。静摩擦系数大于动摩擦,静摩擦可提供更大的牵引力。

5. 动摩擦:轮胎在路面上打滑。动态摩擦系数较低,所以牵引力较小。

很简单,车轮发生滑移时,作用在轮胎上的力超过到轮胎的牵引力。力施加到轮胎的方式有两种:

纵向:纵向力是由发动机或刹车施加于轮胎,用于汽车加速或减速。

横向:当汽车曲线行驶时产生侧向力。它使汽车改变方向——说到底,轮胎与地面提供横向力。

在干燥路面上,甚至在潮湿的平坦路面上,大多数人开车远远不会达到可以获得的最大牵引力。四轮和全轮驱动系统在低附着力的条件下是最有用的,如雪地、湿滑的坡道上。

四轮驱动可以在各种情况下起到作用。例如:

雪地:推车穿过雪地需要很大的力。力的大小局限于可用牵引力。如果有几英寸厚的雪,大多数两轮驱动车无法在道路上前进,因为在雪地里,每个轮胎牵引力很小。四轮驱动的汽车可以利用所有四个轮胎的牵引力。

越野:在越野条件下,至少有一对轮胎牵引力较小的情况是相当普遍的,如通过水流或泥水坑。对于四轮驱动,另一组仍有牵引力,所以他们可以帮你通过。

爬滑坡:这时需要很大的牵引力。四轮驱动汽车可以利用所有四个轮胎的牵引拉车上坡。

也有一些情况下,四驱与双轮驱动比没有优势。最显著的是,四轮驱动系统不会帮助你在湿滑路面停车。一切都取决于刹车防抱死制动系统(ABS)。

四轮驱动系统部件

四轮驱动系统的主要部件是两个差速器(前、后)和分动箱。此外,分时系统有差速锁,两种类型的系统可能都有先进的电子技术,帮助他们更好利用获得的牵引力。

差速器:一辆车有两个差速器,一个在两个前轮间,另一个在两后轮之间。他们将转矩从驱动轴传输到驱动轮。当转弯时,他们还允许左右车轮以不同的速度旋转。

分动箱

在四轮驱动汽车上该装置将动力分配到前后桥。分时四轮驱动系统的分动箱将前桥驱动轴与后轴驱动轴锁止,使车轮被迫以相同的速度旋转。此类分时系统只能用于低牵引的情况下,因此时轮胎比较容易打滑。在干燥的混凝土路面上,轮胎不易打滑,所以四驱应该脱离以避免运动干涉和轮胎及传动系额外的磨损。有些分动箱在分时系统很常见,还具有另外一组齿轮提供高低挡。低挡时,车辆可能最高时速约为5英里(8公里),但可提供格外大的扭矩给车轮。这让司机可慢慢而平稳地爬很陡的山坡。

差速锁

因所有车轮都连接到轮毂上。分时四轮驱动卡车通常有前桥差速锁。当四轮驱动分离时，差速锁不将前轮与前差速器、半轴(连接差速器到轮毂的半轴)和驱动轴连接起来。这样，速度可以不同，两轮驱动时，半轴和驱动轴停止旋转，以减少部件磨损和扭断，也会节约燃油。

先进的电子技术

很多现代的四轮和全轮驱动车辆，先进的电子元件起关键作用。汽车上ABS系统刹车时可选择性作用开始打滑的车轮上，即制动牵引力控制。另一些汽车具有先进的电子控制的离合器，可以更好地控制扭矩传输给车轮。

基础系统

通常分时系统多用于皮卡和老式SUV，工作原理是这样的：通常车辆由后轮驱动。变速箱与分动箱直连，然后，一个驱动轴传向前桥，一个传给后桥。

当四轮驱动作用时，分动箱锁前后驱动轴，每个轴接收来自发动机的一半扭矩。同时，前轮毂锁止。

先前，我们说最好的四轮驱动系统会向每个车轮输送最佳的扭矩，最适宜的扭矩不会引起车轮打滑。按此标准，系统效率相当低。它传到车轮扭矩的大小不会导致轮胎低牵引而滑移。

Unit 5

Automatic Transmission

扫码获取
扩展视频

The modern automatic transmission consists of many components and systems that are designed to work together in a symphony of clever mechanical, hydraulic and electrical technology that has evolved over the years into what many mechanically inclined individuals consider to be an art form.

Planetary Gear Sets

Automatic transmissions contain many gears in various combinations. In a manual transmission, gears slide along shafts as you move the shift lever from one position to another, engaging various sized gears as required in order to provide the correct gear ratio. In an automatic transmission, however, the gears are never physically moved and are always engaged to the same gears.

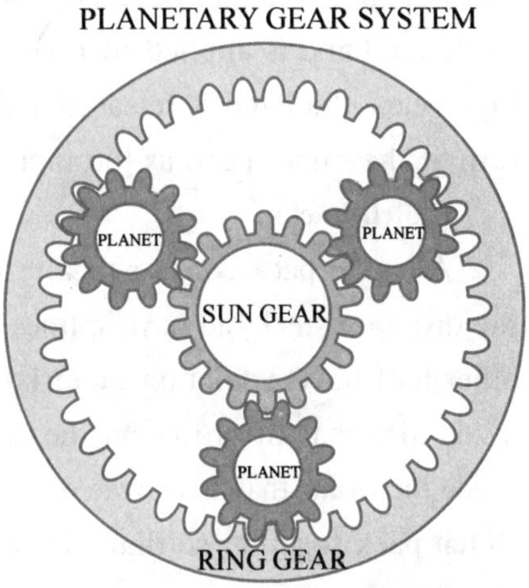

Fig. 5 - 1 planetary gear set model

The basic planetary gear set consists of a sun gear, a ring gear and two or more planet gears, all remaining in constant mesh. The planet gears are connected to each other through a common carrier which allows the gears to spin on shafts called "pinions" which are attached to the carrier.

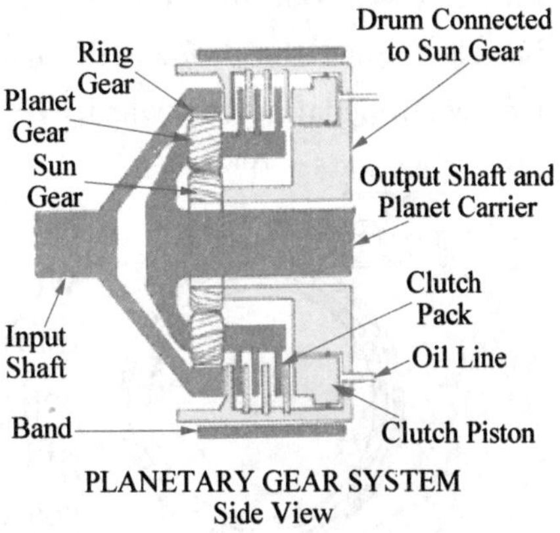

Fig. 5 - 2 side view of planetary gear

One example of a way that this system can be used is by connecting the ring gear to the input shaft coming from the engine, connecting the planet carrier to the output shaft, and locking the sun gear so that it can't move. In this scenario, when we turn the ring gear, the planets will "walk" along the sun gear (which is held stationary) causing the planet carrier to turn the output shaft in the same direction as the input shaft but at a slower speed causing gear reduction (similar to a car in first gear).

If unlock the sun gear and lock any two elements together, this will cause all three elements to turn at the same speed so that the output shaft will turn at the same rate of speed as the input shaft. This is like a car that is in third or high gear. Another way that we can use a planetary gear set is by locking the planet carrier from moving, then applying power to the ring gear which will cause the sun gear to turn in the opposite direction giving us reverse gear.

The clutch pack is used, in this instance, to lock the planet carrier with the sun gear forcing both to turn at the same speed. If both the clutch pack and the band were released, the system would be in neutral. Turning the input shaft would turn the planet gears against the sun gear, but since nothing is holding the sun gear, it will just spin free and have no effect on the output shaft. To place the unit in first gear, the band is applied to hold the sun gear from moving. To shift from first to high gear, the band is released and the clutch is applied causing the output shaft to turn at the same speed as the input shaft.

Clutch Packs

A clutch pack consists of alternating disks that fit inside a clutch drum. Half of the disks are steel and have splines that fit into groves on the inside of the drum. The other half have a friction material bonded to their surface and have splines on the inside edge that fit groves on the outer surface of the adjoining hub. There is a piston inside the drum that is activated by oil pressure at the appropriate time to squeeze the clutch pack together so that the two components become locked and turn as one.

One-Way Clutch

A one-way clutch is a device that will allow a component such as ring gear to turn freely in one direction but not in the other. This effect is just like that of a bicycle, where the pedals will turn the wheel when pedaling forward, but will spin free when pedaling backward.

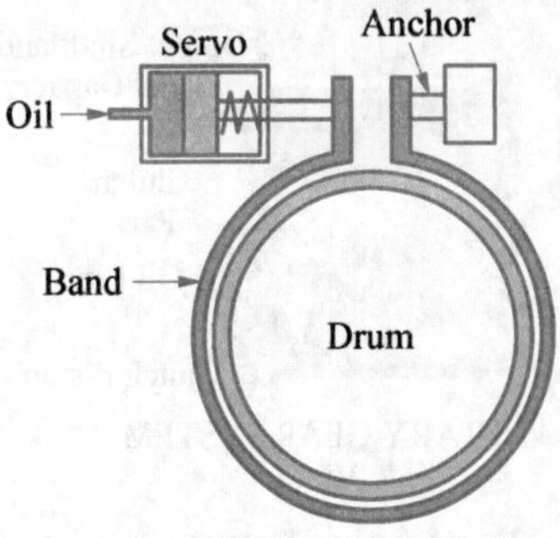

Fig. 5-3 oil servo band

A common place where a one-way clutch is used is in first gear when the shifter is in the drive position. When you begin to accelerate from a stop, the transmission starts out in first gear. But have you ever noticed what happens if you release the gas while it is still in first gear? The vehicle continues to coast as if you were in neutral. Now, shift into Low gear instead of Drive. When you let go of the gas in this case, you will feel the engine slow you down just like a standard shift car. The reason for this is that in Drive, a one-way clutch is used whereas in Low, a clutch pack or a band is used.

Bands

A band is a steel strap with friction material bonded to the inside surface. One end of the band is anchored against the transmission case while the other end is connected to a servo. At the appropriate time hydraulic oil is sent to the servo under pressure to tighten the band around the drum to stop the drum from turning.

Torque Converter

On automatic transmissions, the torque converter takes the place of the clutch found on standard shift vehicles. A torque converter is a large doughnut shaped device (10″ to 15″ in diameter) that is mounted between the engine and the transmission. It consists of three internal elements that work together to transmit power to the transmission. The three elements of the torque converter are the Pump, the Turbine, and the Stator. The pump is mounted directly to the converter housing which in turn is bolted directly to the engine's crankshaft and turns at engine speed. The turbine is inside the housing and is connected directly to the input shaft of the transmission providing power to move the vehicle. The stator is mounted to a one-way clutch so that it can spin freely in one direction but not in the other. Each of the three elements have fins mounted in them to precisely direct the flow of oil through the converter.

With the engine running, transmission fluid is pulled into the pump section and is pushed outward by centrifugal force until it reaches the turbine section which starts it turning. The fluid continues in a circular motion back towards the center of the turbine where it enters the stator. If the turbine is moving considerably slower than the pump, the fluid will make contact with the front of the stator fins which push the stator into the one way clutch and prevent it from turning. With the stator stopped, the fluid is directed by the stator fins to re-enter the pump at a "helping" angle providing a torque increase. As the speed of the turbine catches up with the pump, the fluid starts hitting the stator blades on the back-side causing the stator to turn in the same direction as the pump and turbine. As the speed increases, all three elements begin to turn at approximately the same speed.

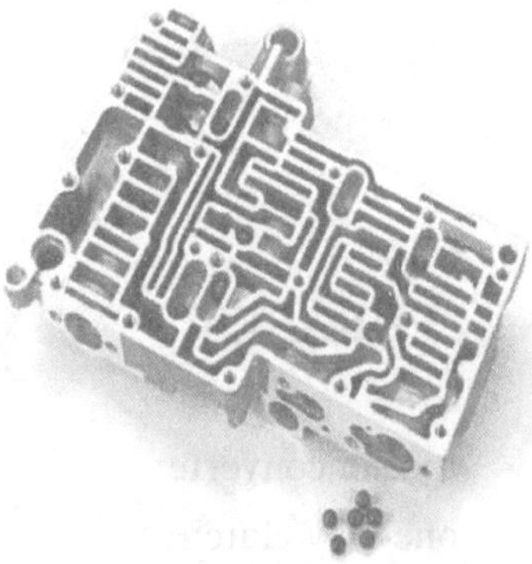

Fig. 5 - 4 hydraulic valve

Hydraulic System

The hydraulic system is a complex maze of

passages and tubes that sends transmission fluid under pressure to all parts of the transmission and torque converter. Transmission fluid serves a number of purposes including: shift control, general lubrication and transmission cooling.

Computer Controls

The computer uses sensors on the engine and transmission to detect such things as throttle position, vehicle speed, engine speed, engine load, brake pedal position, etc. Once the computer receives this information, it then sends signals to a solenoid pack inside the transmission. Computerized transmissions even learn your driving style and constantly adapt to it so that every shift is timed precisely when you would need it.

Advantage to these "smart" transmissions is that they have a self diagnostic mode which can detect a problem early and warn you with an indicator light on the dash. A technician can then plug test equipment in and retrieve a list of trouble codes that will help pinpoint where the problem is.

NEW WORDS

symphony	[ˈsɪmfəni]	*n*.	交响乐
turbine	[ˈtəːbain]	*n*.	涡轮
stator	[ˈsteɪtə]	*n*.	导轮
doughnut	[ˈdəunʌt]	*n*.	圆环
band	[bænd]	*n*.	制动带
scenario	[səˈnɑːriəu]	*n*.	情况
pinion	[ˈpinjən]	*n*.	小齿轮
neutral	[ˈnjuːtrəl]	*v*.	空挡
accelerate	[əkˈseləreɪt]	*v*.	加速
imperceptible	[ˌɪmpəˈseptəbl]	*adj*.	觉察不到的
flange	[flændʒ]	*n*.	法兰盘
governor	[ˈgʌvənə]	*n*.	调节器

PHRASES

torque converter	液力变矩器
one-way clutch	单向离合器
planetary gear set	行星齿轮组

sun gear	太阳轮
planetary gear	行星齿轮
ring gear	齿圈
planet carrier	行星架
vacuum modulator	真空调节器
manual transmission	手动变速器
clutch pack	离合器组件
clutch plate	离合器片
clutch disc	离合器摩擦片
centrifugal force	离心力
lockup clutch	锁止离合器
shift valve	换挡阀
manual valve	手动阀
solenoid pack	电磁阀组件

REVIEW QUESTIONS

(1) What are the compents of thc basic planetary gear set?

(2) What is the meaning of the "one-way clutch"?

(3) What is the function of the bands?

(4) What are the three internal elements of the torque converter?

(5) What is the result of connecting the ring gear to the input shaft coming from the engine, connecting the planet carrier to the output shaft, and locking the sun gear?

REFERENCE TRANSLATION

自动变速器

现代自动变速器由许多部件和系统构成,设计成机械液力和电子控制协调作用,这些花费了许多技术人员各自的思想才形成了这样一种艺术化形式。

行星齿轮组

自动变速器有许多不同的齿轮组合。手动变速箱中齿轮沿轴向滑动,当你将换挡杆从一个位置移动到另一个位置,使大小不同的齿轮按要求进行啮合,提供正确的传动比。然而在自动变速器中,齿轮不移动,并保持啮合。

基本的行星齿轮装置由一个太阳轮,齿圈和两个或两个以上的行星齿轮构成,所有齿轮保持常啮合。行星齿轮通过一个共同的行星架彼此连接,使齿轮绕轴旋转称为"小齿轮”，小齿轮都安装在行星架上。

一种用法是，该系统大齿圈连接到来自发动机的输入轴，行星架与输出轴相连，并锁定太阳齿轮（即固定），使其不能移动。在这种情况下，当我们转动齿圈，行星将沿着太阳轮“走”，使行星架转动输出轴和输入轴在同一方向，但速度较慢，导致齿轮减速（类似汽车在第一挡）。

如果解开太阳轮并锁定其他两个元件，这将导致所有三个元件速度相同，从而使输出轴速度与输入轴相同，这就像一辆汽车处于三挡或高挡。另一种行星齿轮组使用方式是移动行星架固定，然后将动力施加到齿圈，使太阳齿轮转向相反的方向，可得到倒挡。

在这种情况下使用离合器组件将行星架与太阳轮锁止，迫使它们以相同的转速转动。如松开离合器组件和抱闸带，系统处于空挡。转动输入轴会带动行星齿轮围绕太阳轮转动，但因为太阳轮没有锁止，它只是空转，对输出轴没有传力。如在一挡，用抱闸带固定太阳轮防止转动。从一挡换到高挡，带松开，离合器组件起作用，从而使输出轴以输入轴相同的速度转动。

离合器组件

离合器由交替安装在离合器鼓内部的盘片组成。一半的盘片是钢盘，具有外花键装在离合器鼓内花键上。另一半盘片表面黏合有摩擦材料，内侧边缘有花键啮合在连接轴外表面键槽上。在适当的时候，液压油将离合器毂内活塞挤压，使组件连接在一起，钢片摩擦片两元件锁成一体转动。

单向离合器

单向离合器是这样一种装置，允许一个组件如大齿圈向一个方向自由转动而反过来不行。这种效果就像是一辆自行车，踏板前蹬时车轮前进，但后蹬时则自由旋转。

单向离合器常用于在第一挡，此时排挡杆在行驶位置。当你从停止开始加速，变速箱从一挡开始，但你有没有注意到，当它仍然是在第一挡，如果你松开油门踏板，会发生什么？如在空挡汽车会继续滑行。现在，从行驶挡切换到低速挡。如在这种情况下松开油门踏板，你会感觉到发动机慢慢降下速度，就像手动挡一样。这是因为在行驶挡时，单向离合器起作用，而在低挡，离合器组件和抱闸起作用。

闸带

闸带是一种钢带，内表面黏合有摩擦材料，闸带一端固定在变速器壳体上，另一端连接到伺服油缸。在适当的时候液压油送入伺服缸以收紧闸带防止滚筒转动。

液力变矩器

在自动变速器汽车上，液力变矩器位于手动变速器汽车离合器位置，变矩器是个大圆状装置（直径 10 到 15 英寸），装在发动机与变速箱之间，由三个元件组成，协同配合传递动力给变速器，这三个元件是：泵轮、涡轮与导轮，泵轮与变矩器壳体相连，壳体用螺栓与发动机曲轴直连，与发动机速度相同，涡轮在壳体里面直接与变速器输入轴相连，提供动力驱动汽车，导轮装在单向离合器上，可向一个方向自由转动，而向反方向不能，三个元件都有翘片准确导流。

在发动机运转时，传动液进入泵轮，由离心力向外推，直达涡轮使其转动。流体不断循环运动回到涡轮中心进入导轮。如果涡轮速度低于泵轮很多，液体会接触到定子翘片，推动导轮至单向离合器，防止导轮转动。导轮停止时，流体由导轮翘片导向以期望的角度重新进入泵轮增加扭矩，随着涡轮转速增加到与泵轮相同，液体冲击导轮背面使导轮与泵轮和涡轮同向旋转。随着转速增加，这三个元件开始以大约相同的速度转动。

液压系统

液压系统是一个复杂迷宫式管道，传输液压变速器油到变速器和变矩器各元件，变速器油有多项用途，包括：换挡控制、润滑和变速器冷却。

计算机控制

计算机利用发动机和变速器上的传感器检测诸如油门位置、车速、发动机转速、发动机负荷、制动踏板位置等，一旦计算机接收到这些信息，然后发送信号给变速器内的电磁阀。电脑控制的自动变速器甚至能学会和不断地适应你的驾驶方式，当你需要时换挡会更加及时精确。

这些“智能”变速器的优势是他们有一个自我诊断模式，可以早期发现问题，并用你的仪表板上的指示灯报警。技术员可以插上测试设备，检测出故障代码，将有助于查明问题。

Unit 6

Auto Air Conditioning System

扫码获取
扩展视频

Today, as we drive our automobiles, a great many of us, can enjoy the same comfort levels that we are accustomed to at home and at work. With the push of a button or the slide of a lever, we make the seamless transition from heating to cooling and back again without ever wondering how this change occurs. That is, unless something goes awry.

Fig. 6 - 1 air condition panel

Since the advent of the automotive air conditioning system in the 1940's, many things have undergone extensive change. Improvements, such as computerized automatic temperature control (which allow you to set the desired temperature and have the system adjust automatically) and improvements to overall durability, have added complexity to today's modern air conditioning system. Unfortunately, the days of "do-it-yourself" repair to these systems, is almost a thing of the past.

To add to the complications, we now have tough environmental regulations that govern the very simplest of tasks, such as recharging the system with refrigerant R12 commonly referred to as Freon ® (Freon is the trade name for the refrigerant R-12, that was manufactured by DuPont). Extensive scientific studies have proven the damaging effects of this refrigerant to our ozone layer, and its manufacture has been banned by the U. S. and many other countries that have joined together to sign the Montreal Protocol, a landmark agreement that was introduced in the 1980's

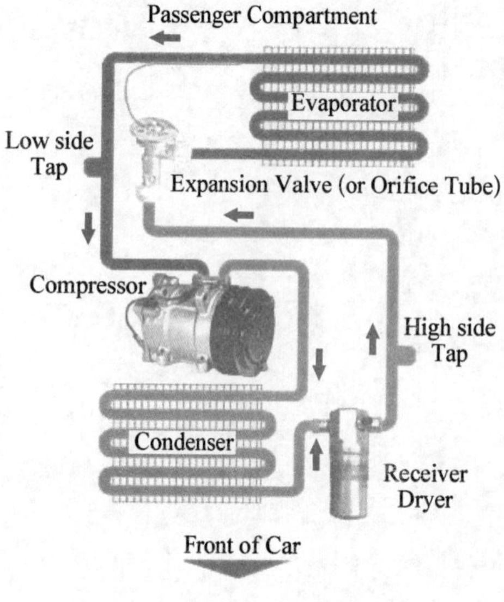

Fig. 6 - 2 air condition principle

to limit the production and use of chemicals known to deplete the ozone layer.

Now more than ever, your auto mechanic is at the mercy of this new environmental legislation. Not only is he required to be certified to purchase refrigerant and repair your air conditioner, his shop must also incur the cost of purchasing expensive dedicated equipment that insures the capture of these ozone depleting chemicals. Simply put, if your mechanic has to spend more to repair your vehicle—he will have to charge you more. Basic knowledge of your air conditioning system is important, as this will allow you to make a more informed decision on your repair options.

Should a major problem arise from your air conditioner, you may encounter new terminology. Words like "retrofit" and "alternative refrigerant" are now in your mechanics glossary. You may be given an option of "retrofitting", as opposed to merely repairing and recharging with Freon. Retrofitting involves making the necessary changes to your system, which will allow it to use the new industry accepted, "environmentally friendly" refrigerant, R-134a. This new refrigerant has a higher operating pressure, therefore, your system, dependant on age, may require larger or more robust parts to counter its inherent high pressure characteristics. This, in some cases, will add significantly to the final cost of the repair. And if not performed properly, may reduce cooling efficiency which equates to higher operating costs and reduced comfort.

Vehicles are found to have primarily three different types of air conditioning systems. While each of the three types differ, the concept and design are very similar to one another. The most common components which make up these automotive systems are the following:

COMPRESSOR, CONDENSER, EVAPORATOR, ORIFICE TUBE, THERMAL EXPANSION VALVE, RECEIVER-DRIER, ACCUMULATOR. Note: if your car has an Orifice Tube, it will not have a Thermal Expansion Valve as these two devices serve the same purpose. Also, you will either have a Receiver-Dryer or an Accumulator, but not both.

Compressor

Commonly referred to as the heart of the system, the compressor is a belt driven pump that is fastened to the engine. It is responsible for compressing and transferring refrigerant gas. The A/C system is split into two sides, a high pressure side and a low pressure side; defined as discharge and suction. Since the compressor is basically a pump, it must have an intake side and a discharge side. The intake, or suction side, draws in refrigerant gas from the outlet of the evaporator. In some cases it does this via the accumulator.

Once the refrigerant is drawn into the suction side, it is compressed and sent to the condenser, where it can then transfer the heat that is absorbed from the inside of the vehicle.

Condenser

This is the area in which heat dissipation occurs. The condenser, in many cases, will have much the same appearance as the radiator in your car as the two have very similar functions. The condenser is designed to radiate heat. Its location is usually in front of the radiator, but in some cases, due to aerodynamic improvements to the body of a vehicle, its location may differ. Condensers must have good air flow anytime the system is in operation. On rear wheel drive vehicles, this is usually accomplished by taking advantage of your existing engine's cooling fan. On front wheel drive vehicles, condenser air flow is supplemented with one or more electric cooling fan(s).

As hot compressed gasses are introduced into the top of the condenser, they are cooled off. As the gas cools, it condenses and exits the bottom of the condenser as a high pressure liquid.

Evaporator

Located inside the vehicle, the evaporator serves as the heat absorption component. The evaporator provides several functions. Its primary duty is to remove heat from the inside of your vehicle. A secondary benefit is dehumidification. As warmer air travels through the aluminum fins of the cooler evaporator coil, the moisture contained in the air condenses on its surface. Dust and pollen passing through stick to its wet surfaces and drain off to the outside. On humid days you may have seen this as water dripping from the bottom of your vehicle. Rest assured this is perfectly normal.

The ideal temperature of the evaporator is 32° Fahrenheit or 0° Celsius. Refrigerant enters the bottom of the evaporator as a low pressure liquid. The warm air passing through the evaporator fins causes the refrigerant to boil (refrigerants have very low boiling points). As the refrigerant begins to boil, it can absorb large amounts of heat. This heat is then carried off with the refrigerant to the outside of the vehicle. Several other components work in conjunction with the evaporator. As mentioned above, the ideal temperature for an evaporator coil is 32° F. Temperature and pressure regulating devices must be used to control its temperature. While there are many variations of devices used, their main functions are the same: keeping pressure in the evaporator low and keeping the evaporator from freezing; A frozen evaporator coil will not absorb as much heat.

Pressure Regulating Devices

Controlling the evaporator temperature can be accomplished by controlling refrigerant pressure and flow into the evaporator. Many variations of pressure regulators have been introduced since the 1940's. Listed below, are the most commonly found.

Orifice Tube

The orifice tube, probably the most commonly used, can be found in most GM and Ford models. It is located in the inlet tube of the evaporator, somewhere between the outlet of the condenser and the inlet of the evaporator. This point can be found in a properly functioning system by locating the area between the outlet of the condenser and the inlet of the evaporator that suddenly makes the change from hot to cold. Most of the orifice tubes in use today measure approximately three inches in length and consist of a small brass tube, surrounded by plastic, and covered with a filter screen at each end. It is not uncommon for these tubes to become clogged with small debris. While inexpensive, usually between three to five dollars, the labor to replace one involves recovering the refrigerant, opening the system up, replacing the orifice tube, evacuating and then recharging. With this in mind, it might make sense to install a larger pre-filter in front of the orifice tube to minimize the risk of of this problem reoccurring. Some Ford models have a permanently affixed orifice tube in the liquid line. These can be cut out and replaced with a combination filter/orifice assembly.

Thermal Expansion Valve

Another common refrigerant regulator is the thermal expansion valve, or TXV. Commonly used on import and aftermarket systems, this type of valve can sense both temperature and pressure, and is very efficient at regulating refrigerant flow to the evaporator. Several variations of this valve are commonly found. Another example of a thermal expansion valve is Chrysler's "H block" type. This type of valve is usually located at the firewall, between the evaporator inlet and outlet tubes and the liquid and suction lines. These types of valves, although efficient, have some disadvantages over orifice tube systems. Like orifice tubes these valves can become clogged with debris, but also have small moving parts that may stick and malfunction due to corrosion.

Receiver-Drier

The receiver-drier is used on the high side of systems that use a thermal expansion valve. This type of metering valve requires liquid refrigerant. To ensure that the valve gets liquid refrigerant, a receiver is used. The primary function of the receiver-drier is to separate gas and liquid. The secondary purpose is to remove moisture and filter out dirt. The receiver-drier usually has a sight glass in the top. This sight glass is often used to charge the system. Under normal operating conditions, vapor bubbles should not be visible in the sight glass. The use of the sight glass to charge the system is not recommended in R-134a systems as oil that has separated from the refrigerant can be mistaken for bubbles. This type of mistake can lead to a dangerous overcharged condition. There are variations of receiver-driers and several different desiccant materials are in use. Some of the moisture removing desiccants found within are not compatible with R-134a. The desiccant type is usually identified on a sticker that is affixed to the receiver-drier. Newer receiver-driers use desiccant type XH-7 and are compatible with both R-12 and R-134a refrigerants.

Accumulator

Accumulators are used on systems that accommodate an orifice tube to meter refrigerants into the evaporator. It is connected directly to the evaporator outlet and stores excess liquid refrigerant. Introduction of liquid refrigerant into a compressor can do serious damage. Compressors are designed to compress gas not liquid. The chief role of the accumulator is to isolate the compressor from any damaging liquid refrigerant. Accumulators, like receiver-driers, also remove debris and moisture from a system. It is a good idea to replace the accumulator each time the system is opened up for major repair and anytime moisture and/or debris is of concern. Moisture is enemy number one for your A/C system. Moisture in a system mixes with refrigerant and forms a corrosive acid. When in doubt, it may be to your advantage to change the accumulator or receiver in your system. While this may be a temporary discomfort for your wallet, it is of long term benefit to your air conditioning system.

NEW WORDS

awry	[əˈraɪ]	*adj*.	错误的
durability	[ˌdjuərəˈbɪlətɪ]	*n*.	耐久力
landmark	[ˈlændmɑːk]	*n*.	里程碑
purchase	[ˈpɜːtʃəs]	*v*.	购买
retrofit	[ˈretrəufɪt]	*v*.	翻新
refrigerant	[rɪˈfrɪdʒərənt]	*n*.	制冷剂
mechanic	[məˈkænɪk]	*n*.	技工，机修工
compressor	[kəmˈpresə]	*n*.	空气压缩机
condenser	[kənˈdensə]	*n*.	冷凝器
evaporator	[ɪˈvæpəˌreɪtə]	*n*.	蒸发器
dehumidification	[ˈdiːhju(ː)mɪdɪfɪˈkeɪʃn]	*n*.	除去湿气

moisture	[ˈmɔɪstʃə]	*n*.	潮湿、湿气
fahrenheit	[ˈfærənhaɪt]	*n*.	华氏温度
dimple	[ˈdɪmpl]	*n*.	旋涡
accumulator	[əˈkjuːmjəleɪtə]	*n*.	储液器
deplete	[dɪˈpliːt]	*v*.	耗尽

PHRASES

automotive air conditioning system A/C	汽车空调系统
trade name	商标，商品名
ozone layer	大气层
orifice tube	节流管
thermal expansion valve	热膨胀阀
receive-drier	干燥器
rear wheel drive vehicle	后轮驱动汽车
engine's cooling fan	发动机冷却风扇

REVIEW QUESTIONS

(1) What are the most common components of the A/C system?

(2) What is the heart of the A/C system?

(3) What is the function of the evaporator?

(4) What is the function of the receiver-drier?

REFERENCE TRANSLATION

汽车空调系统

我们现在开车，很多人都可以享受我们习惯了的在家里和在工作时同样的舒适程度。按下键或是滑动一下滑杆，我们就可以不知不觉地进行制热到制冷或反过来的连续转换，除非什么部件发生故障。

自从1940年代以来的汽车空调系统出现，很多事情都发生了广泛的变化。如电脑自动温度控制(允许你设置所需的温度并由系统自动调节)和整体的耐久性的改进，增加了现代空调系统的复杂性。不幸的是，“自己动手”修复这些系统的时代几乎已是过去。

更复杂的是，即使是非常简单的任务，现在也受严格的环境法规管理，如给空调添加常见的制冷剂 R12，也称为氟利昂（氟利昂为制冷剂®R－12，是由杜邦公司制造的商品名）。广泛的科学研究已经证明制冷剂对臭氧层有破坏作用，其制造商已经被美国和其他许多国家联合起来签署蒙特利尔协议加以禁止，这是 1980 年代一个里程碑式的协议，旨在限制生产和使用消耗臭氧层的化学物质。

现在比以往任何时候，汽车修理工更受新环境法管制。他不仅需要证书才可购买制冷剂和修理空调，还必须承担购买昂贵的专用设备费用，确保回收这些消耗臭氧层的化学物质。简单地说，如果你的修理工必须花更多钱来修车——他会收费更高。了解空调系统的基本知识是重要的，因为这会让你在维修空调做选择时做出更明智的决定。

如你的空调出现大问题，你可能会遇到新的术语。修理工会说出如“改造”和“替代制冷剂”等术语。你可以选择“改造”，而不是仅仅修复和充注氟利昂。改造需对空调系统做出必要的改变，以使用适应新的行业标准需求的环保制冷剂 R－134a。这种新的制冷剂具有较高的操作压力，因此，您的系统，依据工作年限，可能需要更高强度的元件以应对其固有的高压特性。在某些情况下，这将大大增加维修成本。且如果操作不正确，可能会降低冷却效率，也就是增加用车成本，降低舒适性。

有三种不同类型的空调系统，每种各有不同，但它们的基本原理与设计形式非常相似。组成空调系统最常见的组件如下：压缩机，冷凝器，蒸发器，节流管，热膨胀阀，干燥器、储液器。注：如果你的车有节流管，它将不会有热膨胀阀，因这两个元件作用相同。同样，或有干燥器或储液器，但不会两者皆有。

压缩机

压缩机通常被称为系统的心脏，是一种皮带驱动泵，与发动机相连。它负责压缩和输送气态制冷剂。A/C 系统分成两侧，高压侧和低压侧；也定义为排气侧和吸气侧。由于压缩机基本上是一个泵，它必须有一个进气侧和排气侧。进气或吸入侧，吸入蒸发器出口的制冷剂气体。在某些情况下，它通过储液器吸入制冷剂气体。

一旦制冷剂被吸入到吸入侧，它被压缩传送到冷凝器，然后就传送从车内吸收的热量。

冷凝器

热量在此散发，在许多情况下冷凝器外观与汽车散热器相同，两者功能非常相似。冷凝器是设计用来散热的。它通常位于散热器前面，但有时由于对车辆的车身空气动力学的改进，它的位置可能会有所不同。冷凝器必须在系统运行时有良好的空气流通。在后轮驱动的车辆，这通常是通过利用现有的发动机冷却风扇完成。在前轮驱动的车辆，冷凝器的空气流动辅助以一个或多个电动冷却风扇。

随着热压缩气体引入冷凝器顶部，气体冷却下来。当气体冷却后，就会冷凝并从冷凝器底部出口排出高压液体。

蒸发器

蒸发器位于车内，是热吸收部件。蒸发器提供多种功能。其主要职责是去除你车内的热气。第二个好处是除湿。当暖空气流经蒸发器盘管的铝翅片，空气中的水分将凝结在其表面。灰尘和花粉粘在其潮湿的表面而被排除在车外。潮湿的日子里你可以看到汽车底部滴水，放心，这是完全正常。

蒸发器的理想温度是32华氏度或0摄氏度。制冷剂进入蒸发器的底部时为低压液体。温暖的空气通过蒸发器使制冷剂沸腾(制冷剂具有非常低的沸点)。当制冷剂开始沸腾，它能吸收大量的热。制冷剂带着热量排出车外。还有其他几个元件与蒸发器连接。如上所述，蒸发器盘管的理想温度是32华氏温度，温度与压力调节装置必须用来控制其温度。调节装置种类很多，其主要功能是相同的：保持蒸发器低压并防止蒸发器结冰；结冰的蒸发器不会吸收太多的热量。

压力调节装置

通过控制制冷剂压力和蒸发器流量来控制蒸发器温度，从1940年代起，出现很多种压力调节装置，以下列出的是最常见的几种。

节流管

节流管，可能是最常用的，安装在大多数通用汽车和福特汽车上。它位于蒸发器的入口管，在冷凝器的出口与蒸发器入口之间某个位置。在正常运作的系统中，此处突然从热变冷，位于冷凝器的出口与蒸发器入口间的区域。今天大多数使用的节流管大约三英寸长，是由一个被塑料包围，两端都有滤网的小铜管构成。这些管被小碎片堵塞的情况并不少见。虽然便宜，通常是三到五美元之间，其维修涉及回收制冷剂，打开系统，更换节流管，抽真空，然后再充注。考虑到这一点，通常在孔口管的前面安装一个更大的预过滤器，最大限度减少这一问题再次发生的风险。一些福特车型的液体管路中有一个固定孔管。这些可以被组合过滤器/节流孔组件切断和更换。

热膨胀阀

另一个常见的制冷剂调节器是热膨胀阀热力或TXV。这种类型的阀门常见于进口车和汽车后市场，能够感知温度和压力，可非常有效地调节到蒸发器的制冷剂流。本阀常见几种形式。另一种膨胀阀是克莱斯勒的"H座"型。这种类型的阀门通常位于防火墙上，蒸发器的入口和出口管和液体分界线之间。这些类型的阀门虽然有效，与节流管系统比有一些缺点。如节流孔这些阀门不但可以被碎片堵塞，而且也会有小颗粒流过去，可能会引起腐蚀和故障。

干燥器

干燥器适用于系统使用热力膨胀阀的高压侧。这种类型的膨胀阀需要液态制冷剂。使用接收器确保阀门得到的是液体制冷剂。干燥器的主要功能是分离气体和液体。次要目的是去除水分和过滤掉污垢。干燥器顶部通常有透视玻璃。通常利用此玻璃充注制冷剂。在正常工作时，透视玻璃上不应看见气泡。在R－134a系统中不建议使用透视玻璃充注，因为机油从制冷剂分离可能被误认为是气泡。这种类型的错误可能会导致一种过度充注状态。干燥器有多种，干燥剂材料也有多种，其中有些被发现的去水分干燥剂与R－134a不兼容。干燥剂类型通常以标签贴在干燥机上。新型干燥器使用xh－7型号干燥剂，并与R－12和R－134a制冷剂兼容。

储液器

储液器用于计量节流孔进入蒸发器的制冷剂量的空洞系统，它直接连接到蒸发器出口并储存多余的液态制冷剂。液体制冷剂进入压缩机会造成严重损害。设计压缩机是为了压缩气体而不是液体。储液器的主要作用是将压缩机与任何有害液体制冷剂隔离开。储液器如同干燥器,也可去除系统的杂质和水分。最好每次在打开系统做维修时更换蓄液器、去除水分和杂质。水分是A/C系统的头号敌人。在一个系统中的水分与制冷剂混合并形成腐蚀性酸。如怀疑有酸,最好更换系统储液器或干燥器。虽然这可能暂时会花点费用,但长期有益于你的空调系统。

Unit 7

Antilock Brake System

扫码获取
扩展视频

The ABS is a four-wheel system that prevents wheel lock-up by automatically modulating the brake pressure during an emergency stop. By preventing the wheels from locking, it enables the driver to maintain steering control and to stop in the shortest possible distance under most conditions.

During normal braking, the ABS and non-ABS brake pedal feel will be the same.

During ABS operation, a pulsation can be felt in the brake pedal, accompanied by a fall and then rise in brake pedal height and a clicking sound.

Vehicles with ABS are equipped with a pedal-actuated, dual-brake system. The hydraulic system consists of the following:

1. ABS hydraulic control valves and electronic control unit
2. Power brake booster
3. Brake master cylinder
4. Necessary brake tubes and hoses

The anti-lock brake system consists of the following components:

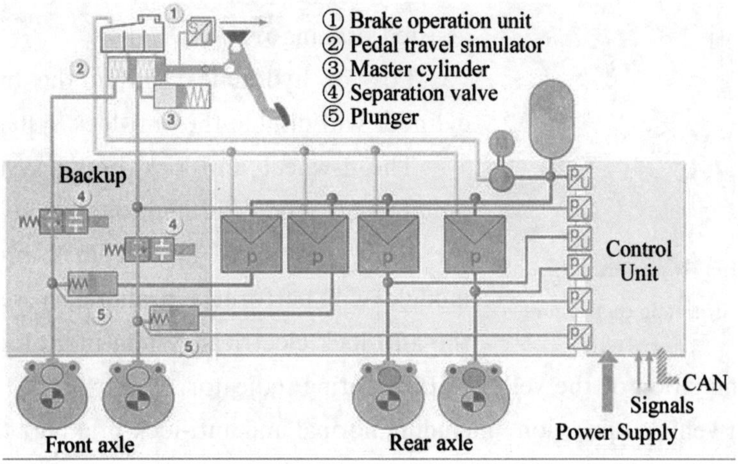

Fig. 7-1　ABS system

1. Hydraulic Control Unit (HCU)

2. Anti-lock brake control module

3. Front anti-lock brake sensors / Rear anti-lock brake sensors

Anti-lock Brake System (ABS) operates as follows:

When the brakes are applied, fluid is forced from the brake master cylinder outlet ports to the HCU inlet ports. This pressure is transmitted through four normally open solenoid valves contained inside the HCU, then through the outlet ports of the HCU to each wheel.

The primary (rear) circuit of the brake master cylinder feeds the front brakes.

The secondary (front) circuit of the brake master cylinder feeds the rear brakes.

If the anti-lock brake control module senses a wheel is about to lock, based on anti-lock brake sensor data, it closes the normally open solenoid valve for that circuit. This prevents any more fluid from entering that circuit.

The anti-lock brake control module then looks at the anti-lock brake sensor signal from the affected wheel again.

If that wheel is still decelerating, it opens the solenoid valve for that circuit. Once the affected wheel comes back up to speed, the anti-lock brake control module returns the solenoid valves to their normal condition allowing fluid flow to the affected brake.

The anti-lock brake control module monitors the electromechanical components of the system.

Fig. 7-2 hydraulic control unit

Malfunction of the anti-lock brake system will cause the anti-lock brake control module to shut off or inhibit the system. However, normal power-assisted braking remains.

Loss of hydraulic fluid in the brake master cylinder will disable the anti-lock system.

The 4-wheel anti-lock brake system is self-monitoring. When the ignition switch is turned to the RUN position, the anti-lock brake control module will perform a preliminary self-check on the anti-lock electrical system indicated by a three second illumination of the yellow ABS wanting indicator.

During vehicle operation, including normal and anti-lock braking, the anti-lock brake control module monitors all electrical anti-lock functions and some hydraulic operations.

Each time the vehicle is driven, as soon as vehicle speed reaches approximately 20 km/h (12 mph), the anti-lock brake control module turns on the pump motor for approximately one-half second. At this time, a mechanical noise may be heard. This is a normal function of the self-check by the anti-lock brake control module.

When the vehicle speed goes below 20 km/h (12 mph), the ABS turns off.

Most malfunctions of the anti-lock brake system and traction control system, if equipped, will cause the yellow ABS warning indicator to be illuminated.

The system uses three basic components to control hydraulic pressure to the rear brakes. These components are:

Electronic Brake Control Module

Anti-Lock Pressure Valve

Vehicle Speed Sensor

ELECTRONIC BRAKE CONTROL MODULE:

The EBCM mounted on a bracket next to the master cylinder, contains a microprocessor and software for system operation.

ANTI-LOCK PRESSURE VALVE:

The Anti-Lock Pressure Valve (APV) is mounted to the combination valve under the master cylinder, has an isolation valve to maintain or increase hydraulic pressure and a dump valve to reduce hydraulic pressure.

VEHICLE SPEED SENSOR:

The Vehicle Speed Sensor (VSS) located on the left rear of the transmission on two-wheel drive trucks and on the transfer case of four-wheel drive vehicles, produces an AC voltage signal that varies in frequency according to the output shaft speed.

On some vehicles the VSS is located in the rear differential.

BASE BRAKING MODE:

During normal braking, the EBCM receives a signal from the stop lamp switch and begins to monitor the vehicle speed line. The isolation valve is open and the dump valve is seated. This allows fluid under pressure to pass through the APV and travel to the rear brake channel. The reset switch does not move because hydraulic pressure is equal on both sides.

ANTILOCK BRAKING MODE:

During a brake application the EBCM compares vehicle speed to the program built into it. When it senses a rear wheel lock-up condition, it operates the anti-lock pressure valve to keep the rear wheels from locking up. To do this the EBCM uses a three-step cycle:

Pressure Maintain; Pressure Decrease; Pressure Increase;

PRESSURE MAINTAIN:

During pressure maintain the EBCM energizes the isolation solenoid to stop the flow of fluid from the master cylinder to the rear brakes. The reset switch moves when the difference between the master cylinder line pressure and the rear brake channel pressure becomes great enough. If this happens, it grounds the EBCM logic circuit.

PRESSURE DECREASE:

During pressure decrease the EBCM keeps the isolation solenoid energized and energizes the dump solenoid. The dump valve moves off its seat and fluid under pressure moves into the accumulator. This action reduces rear pipe pressure preventing rear lock-up. The reset switch grounds to tell the EBCM that pressure decrease has taken place.

PRESSURE INCREASE:

During pressure increase the EBCM de-energizes the dump and isolation solenoids. The dump valve reseats and holds the stored fluid in the accumulator. The isolation valve opens and allows the fluid from the master cylinder to flow past it and increase pressure to the rear brakes. The reset switch moves back to its original position by spring force. This action signals the EBCM that pressure decrease has ended and driver applied pressure resumes.

SYSTEM SELF-TEST:

When the ignition switch is turned "ON," the EBCM performs a system self-test. It checks its internal and external circuit and performs a function test by cycling the isolation and dump valves. The EBCM then begins its normal operation if no malfunctions are detected.

Brake pedal pulsation and occasional rear tire "chirping" are normal during ABS operation. The road surface and severity of the braking maneuver determine how much these will occur. Since these systems only control the rear wheels, it is still possible to lock the front wheels during certain severe braking conditions.

SPARE TIRE:

Using the spare tire supplied with the vehicle will not affect the performance of the RWAL or system.

REPLACEMENT TIRES:

Tire size can affect the performance of the RWAL system. Replacement tires must be the same size, load range, and construction on all four wheels.

If there is an ABS failure, the system will revert to normal brake operation so you will not be without brakes. Normally the ABS warning light will turn on and let you know there is a fault. When that light is on it is safe to assume the ABS has switched to normal brake operation and you should drive accordingly.

ABS is a technology that has been in use for many years before it was adapted for automotive use. Aircraft have been using some form of ABS since World War II and it is a tried and true system that can be a great help in avoiding accidents.

NEW WORDS

manufacture	[ˌmænjuˈfæktʃə]	*n.*	制造商
version	[ˈvɜːʃn]	*n.*	版本
specification	[ˌspesɪfɪˈkeɪʃn]	*n.*	参数
modulate	[ˈmɒdjuleɪt]	*vt.*	调整
pulsation	[pʌlˈseɪʃn]	*n.*	跳动、震动
click	[klɪk]	*n.*	滴答声
differential	[ˌdɪfəˈrenʃl]	*n.*	差速器
inertia	[ɪˈnɜːʃə]	*n.*	惯性
decelerate	[ˌdiːˈseləreɪt]	*v.*	减速
inhibit	[ɪnˈhɪbɪt]	*v.*	抑制、约束
collision	[kəˈlɪʒn]	*n.*	碰撞
switch	[swɪtʃ]	*n.*	开关
preliminary	[prɪˈlɪmɪnəri]	*adj.*	初步的
illumination	[ɪˌluːmɪˈneɪʃn]	*n.*	闪烁
malfunction	[ˌmælˈfʌŋkʃn]	*n.*	故障
severe	[sɪˈvɪə]	*adj.*	剧烈的
tire	[ˈtaɪə]	*n.*	轮胎

PHRASES

power brake booster	动力制动助力器
brake master cylinder	制动主缸
hydraulic control unit (HCU)	液压控制单元
traction control system	牵引力控制系统
self-monitoring	自检
dual-brake system	双联制动系统
vehicle Speed Sensor (VSS)	车速传感器
solenoid valve	电磁阀

EBCM	电子制动力控制模块
APV	防抱死压力控制阀
RWAL	后轮防抱死系统
light truck	轻卡

NOTES

REVIEW QUESTIONS

(1) Please introduce the ABS working principle briefly.

(2) How do you feel when the ABS is working?

(3) Does the brake work if the ABS fail to do properly for some reasons?

(4) When does the ABS start to self-test?

(5) Give us a representation about the future of ABS.

REFERENCE TRANSLATION

防抱死制动系统

ABS是在紧急制动时通过自动调整制动力防止车轮抱死的四轮系统，车轮防抱死可使驾驶员保持方向控制、在大多情况下以最短距离停车。

在正常制动时，有无ABS刹车踏板的感觉是一样的。

在ABS作用时，可以在制动踏板感觉脉动，伴随着踏板高度下降再上升和滴答声音。

车辆的ABS都配备了踏板驱动双管路系统。液压系统由以下部分组成：

1. ABS液压控制阀和电子控制单元；
2. 动力制动助力器；
3. 制动主缸；
4. 必要的制动管和软管。

防抱死制动系统由以下部分组成：

1. 液压控制单元(HCU)；
2. 防抱死制动控制模块；
3. 前轮ABS传感器/后轮ABS传感器。

防抱死制动系统(ABS)的工作过程如下：

刹车时，流体从制动主缸出口压出到HCU入口。这种压力是通过包含在HCU的四个常开电磁阀发送，然后通过 HCU 出口到达各个车轮。

第一(后)制动回路供油给前制动器。

第二(前)制动回路供油给后制动器。

如果防抱死制动控制模块检测车轮即将抱死，基于防抱死制动传感器数据，它关闭那条管路常开的电磁阀。这将防止更多流体进入管路。

防抱死制动控制模块再次监控受控车轮防抱死制动传感器信号。

如果车轮仍在减速，会打开该管路的回油电磁阀。一旦受控轮重新速度加快，防抱死制动控制模块使电磁阀返回到其常态，使流体流向受控车轮。

防抱死制动控制模块监控系统的机电元件。

防抱死制动系统的故障将导致防抱死制动控制模块关闭。然而，正常的助力制动仍然起作用。

制动主缸的液压油缺少将使防抱死系统失去作用。

四轮防抱死制动系统可自我监控。当点火开关转到运行位置，防抱死制动控制模块将执行防抱死电气系统自检，黄色 ABS 警告灯闪亮三秒钟。

车辆行驶时，包括正常制动和防抱死制动，防抱死制动控制模块监控所有电子防抱死功能和液压操作。

每次行驶，当车速达到约 20 公里/小时(12 英里)，防抱死制动控制模块开启 ABS 油泵电机约半秒钟。这时，可能会听到机械噪音。这是由防抱死制动控制模块的正常自检功能。

当车速低于 20 公里/小时(12 英里)，ABS 关闭。

防抱死制动系统和牵引力控制系统(如果车上配备的话)的大多数故障会引起黄色 ABS 警告灯点亮。

该系统采用三个基本元件控制液压后轮刹车。这些组件是：

电子制动控制模块

防抱死压力阀

车速传感器

电子制动控制模块：

该模块安装在紧靠主缸的支架上，包含一个微处理器和软件驱动系统。

防抱死压力阀：

防抱死压力阀(APV)安装在主缸下组合阀，有一个隔离阀来维持或增加液压，一个泄压阀来减少液压。

车速传感器：

车速传感器(VSS)安装在两轮驱动车上的变速器左后侧，四轮驱动车辆分动箱上，产生一个交流电压信号，根据输出轴转速改变频率。

有一些车辆的 VSS 位于后差速器上。

基本制动方式：

在正常制动时，EBCM 模块接收来自制动灯开关的信号，并开始监测车辆速度曲线。隔离阀打开，泄压阀常态关闭。这允许流体压力通过 APV 传给后制动通道。复位开关不会工作，因为两侧压力相等。

防抱死制动模式：

制动时，EBCM 模块比较车辆速度与内置程序数据。当它感觉到后轮将要抱死，会打开防抱死压力阀防止后轮锁死。这样做时模块使用了三个步骤的循环：

压力保持；压力降低；压力增加。

压力保持：

在压力保持时，模块激活隔离电磁，阻止流体从主缸流向后轮刹车。当主缸管线压力和后制动管路压力差足够大时复位开关动作。如果发生这种情况，模块逻辑电路与零电位接通。

压力降低：

在压力降低时，模块保持隔离电磁阀通电和也接通泄压阀电磁。泄压阀在压力作用下移动离开阀座和流体进入储液器。这样减少后管路压力，防后轮锁止。复位开关搭铁告诉模块压力正在下降。

压力增加：

在压力增加时，泄压阀和隔离电磁阀断电。泄压阀复位，保持存储在储液器的流体。隔离阀打开，允许刹车液从主缸流过去，增加后轮制动压力。复位开关在弹簧力作用下移回其原始位置。这个动作发信号给模块，压力降低已经结束，驾驶员施加的压力恢复。

系统自检：

打开点火开关时，模块执行系统自检。它会检查其内部和外部电路和执行功能测试，通过循环检测隔离阀和切断阀。如果没有检测到故障，EBCM 才开始其正常运行。

ABS 制动时的制动踏板的脉动和偶尔的后轮胎的“唧唧”是正常的。路面状况和各刹车轻重决定这种情况的出现程度。由于这些系统只控制后轮，它仍然可能在某些急刹车情况锁前轮。

备用轮胎：

使用车辆提供的备胎不会影响后轮刹车和系统的性能。

更换轮胎：

轮胎的尺寸会影响后轮防抱死系统的性能。更换轮胎必须是大小相同，负载范围一致，四只轮胎必需结构一样。

如果出现 ABS 故障，系统将恢复到正常的制动操作，所以你不会没有刹车。通常，ABS 警告灯就会让你知道有故障。当 ABS 灯亮，已切换到正常的制动模式，你可以放心驾驶。

用于汽车之前，ABS 已使用多年。自二战以来，飞机已经使用某种形式的 ABS，无论用于实验还是真正的装备飞机，确实有助于避免事故。

Unit 8

Charging System

扫码获取
扩展视频

The charging system provides the electrical energy a car needs once its engine starts. The charging system does two jobs. First, it provides electrical power for the ignition system and the car's electrical accessories. Second, it replaces the power used by the battery in starting the car. In other words, the charging system maintains the battery's state of charge.

The charging system uses the mechanical energy of the engine to generate electricity. For this reason, the charging system is also called the generating system. The charging system should supply only as much current as the car needs. If the charging system puts too much current into the battery, the battery becomes overcharge. This reduces the life of the battery. Also, this may reduce the life of lights and accessories. If the charging system produces too little electricity, the battery may have a charge too low to start the engine.

The charging system has a battery, an alternator, a regulator, and either an ammeter or an indicator light.

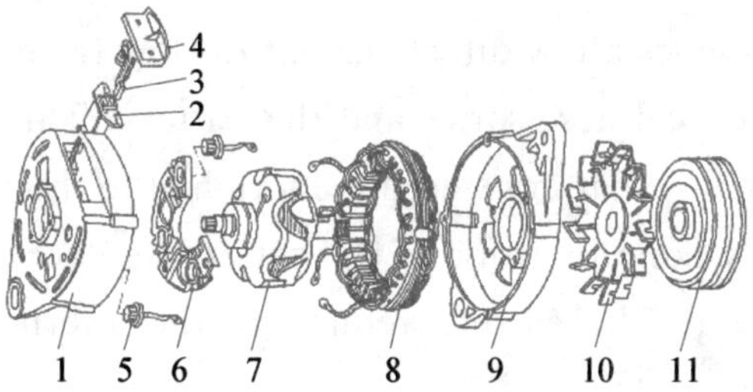

Fig. 8 - 1 structure of alternator

1. rear end frame 2. brush rack 3. brush 4. brush spring cover
5. silicon diode 6. heat radiator 7. rotator 8. stator
9. front frame 10. cooling fan 11. driving wheel

The Alternator

Electricity can be produced by moving a conductor through a magnetic field. The opposite also holds true. By moving the magnetic field and holding the conductor, electricity can be generated in the conductor. This current is called an induced current. This is the basic principle of the alternator, an electromechanical device that changes mechanical energy into electrical energy.

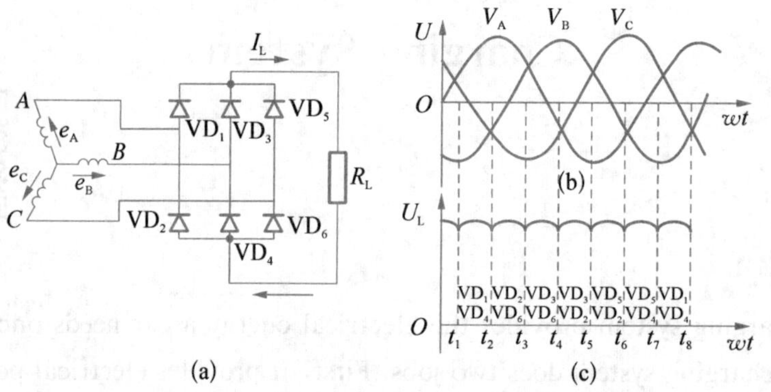

Fig. 8-2 change AC to DC

The alternator has two main parts—a conductor and an electromagnet. The conductor is called the stator and the electromagnet, the rotor.

Changing Alternating Current to Direct Current

The alternator produces alternating current, abbreviated AC. Alternating current is current that flows first in one direction, then in the opposite direction. In contrast, direct current (DC), which the battery produces, flows in only one direction.

The diodes, or rectifiers, of an alternator change AC to DC. These electronic parts allow current to flow easily in one direction. When the current reverses and tries to flow in the opposite direction, the diodes prevent the reverse flow.

Most alternators have six diodes that connect to the wires leading in front of stator. Three positive diodes allow direct current to flow from the alternator's three winding to various electrical accessories and the battery. Three negative diodes let direct current flow from the battery's negative terminal to the alternator. Of course, this current has already done its work in the battery and accessories by the time it returns to the alternator. The current returns to the alternator trough a ground circuit.

The Regulator

The alternator must produce a high current to recharge the battery and provide current to operate various electrical systems. However, as the battery comes up to charge, the amount of current produced by the alternator must decrease. Indeed, if the current does not decrease, the battery will become overcharged.

A part called a voltage regulator regulates the mount of power that alternator produces. It does so by varying the amount of current going to rotor windings or field. If the battery and electrical accessories get more current than they need, the regulator reduces the current going to the rotor. The reduced current is generated in the stator windings. Less power now flows from the alternator to the battery and other electrical accessories. If the battery is not fully charged or the electrical accessories use more current than the alternator produces, the regulator will increase the current going to the rotor field. Then, more power will flow to the battery and electrical accessories.

Some regulators have electromagnetic switches that control the amount of current in the circuit leading to the rotor. When operating properly, these switches let the alternator produce only as much power as the battery and electrical accessories need to do their jobs. Other types of regulators use transistors to control current flow to the alternator.

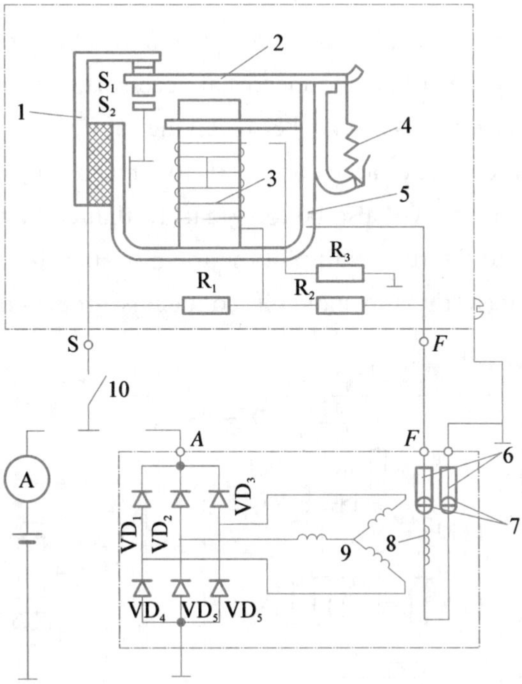

Fig. 8 - 3 the electrical connections for vibrating relay voltage regulator

1. Fixed contact 2. Moving contact 3. Coil 4. Spring 5. Frame 6. Electrical brush 7. Slide ring 8. Magnetic coil 9. Armature winding 10. Ignition switch

There are there types of alternator regulators: vibrating-relay voltage regulators, all-transistor regulators, and integrated microcircuit regulators.

Vibrating-Relay Voltage Regulator

The regulator has two important parts:

(1) A resistance wire that reduces current when electricity flows through it

(2) A relay

The relay controls current flow to the rotor of the alternator. When you turn the ignition key to start the car, current flows from the battery through a closed switch to the B (battery) terminal of the regulator. This current travels through the close contact points of the relay and out the F terminal of the regulator. From there, current goes to the F terminal of the alternator, thus supplying current to the rotor. The current that goes into the field winding of the rotor creates the magnetic field that generates current in the stator windings. The current from the stator windings then flows through the diodes and out the battery terminal of the alternator to the battery. As the battery is charged, battery voltage increases. This increased voltage strengthens the electromagnet in the relay of the regulator. Thus, the electromagnet pulls down the relay and breaks the circuit between the bottom movable contact and the stationary contact.

The resistance wire reduces amount of current reaching the rotor. Thus, less current flows back to the battery and electrical accessories. In spite of this reduced current flow, the battery may still be receiving more current than it needs, especially if a driver uses few accessories. If too much current still reaches the battery, the battery voltage will also be too great. In that case, the high voltage that goes from the battery to the relay will pull the top movable contact down against the stationary contact. Thus, the top movable contact is grounded. Current will flow only to ground.

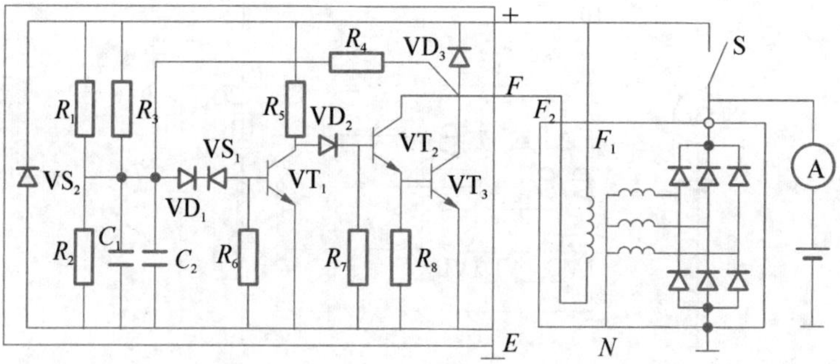

Fig. 8 - 4 all transistor voltage regulator

All-Transistor Regulators

All-transistor regulators are replacing vibrating-relay regulators because all-transistor relays have no moving parts that can wear out.

An all-transistor regulator uses transistors to control the current to the rotor field. A transistor is a tiny electronic switch that can control current flow. The transistors in the regulator operate at set voltage. For example, you might find the regulator set for 13.5 volts. If voltage increases beyond that point, the resistance in the transistor also increases. This decreases current flow to meet the reduced electrical requirements of the car.

If voltage drops below 13.5 volts, the resistance of the transistor decreases. The amount of current flow through the transistor then increases to meet the increased electrical demands of the car.

An all-transistor regulator looks like a vibrating-relay regulator. However, the all-transistor type may be much smaller. Both regulators have the same kinds of connections. In both, current arrives at the regulator and leaves the regulator to go to the rotor winding through the same terminals.

Charging System Maintenance

To keep the alternator, the drive belt must be in good condition and properly tightened. When you do your regular monthly electrical check, twist the alternator drive belt to view the driving surface, or underside, of the belt. If it is cracked or frayed, have it replaced as soon as possible.

There are more than 100 different, commonly-used sizes of drive belts. If you take long trips, always carry spare belts for your car's alternator and coolant pump. Even if you do not want to replace these belts yourself, having the correct spare parts protects you against situations in which a servicc station does not have belts that fit your car.

To check the alternator belt, you can use two techniques. One method is to press down on the belt between the pulleys into which the belt fits. If you can move the belt down ward more than a half-inch from its stationary position, it needs to be tightened. The other test is to try to turn the alternator pulley while the belt is attached. If you can rotate the alternator pulley easily, the belt is too loose.

A loose alternator belt will slip on the pulleys and will not turn the alternator fast enough to keep the battery charged. Eventually, the belt can become "glazed" with a shiny driving surface that may squeal when the engine is accelerated. The heat from slipping on the pulleys dries the rubber, which promotes cracking and belt breakage.

On the other hand, a belt that is too tight will damage the bearings in the units turned by the belt, including the alternator and /or water pump.

For maximum reliability, it is recommended that you change all drive belts every three years or 36, 000 miles, whichever occurs first. Although belts may last longer than three years, changing them at this interval will prevent most problems.

NEW WORDS

ammeter	[ˈæmiːtə]	*n*.	电表
magnetic	[mægˈnetɪk]	*adj*.	磁性的
electromechanical	[ɪˈlektrəumɪˈkænɪkəl]	*adj*.	机电的
integrate	[ˈɪntɪgreɪt]	*vt*.	集成
electromagnet	[ɪˈlektrəumægnət]	*n*.	电磁铁
abbreviate	[əˈbriːvieɪt]	*vt*.	缩写
diode	[ˈdaɪəud]	*n*.	二极管
fray	[freɪ]	*v*.	磨损
squeal	[skwiːl]	*v*.	发出尖叫

PHRASES

charging system	充电系统
movable contact	滑动触点
all transistor voltage regulator	全晶体管电压调节器
vibrating relay voltage regulator	振动继电器电压调节器
alternator drive belt	发电机皮带

REVIEW QUESTIONS

(1) What components are the charging system composed of?

(2) What's the function of voltage regulator?

(3) How to translate AC to DC in charging system?

(4) What's the advantage of all transistor regulator over vibrating one?

(5) How to adjust alternator belt?

REFERENCE TRANSLATION

充电系统

一旦发动机需要起动，充电系统就给汽车提供电能。充电系统有两个作用：第一是提供电能给点火系统和汽车电器附件，第二是提供蓄电池启动汽车时用去的能量，换句话说就是给蓄电池充电保持其电量。

充电系统利用发动机的机械能发电。因此，充电系统也被称为发电系统。充电系统应该提供刚好能满足汽车需要的电流。如果充电系统充太多的电流到电池，电池就过度充电。这降低了电池的寿命。另外，这样可能减少灯及配件的寿命。如果充电系统产生的电流过小，电池可能会因为欠充电而难以启动发动机。

充电系统有一个电池，交流发电机，调节器，和一个电流表或指示灯。

交流发电机

电能可以通过导体在磁场中移动产生。反之也成立。通过移动磁场保持导体不动，导体中就会产生电流。这个电流称为感应电流。这是交流发电机的基本原理，此机电设备转变机械能为电能。

发电机主要有两个部分——导体与电磁铁。导体称为定子，电磁铁为称转子。

交流电转换成直流电

交流发电机产生的交变电流简称AC，交流是一会向一个方向流动，然后再向相反的方向流动。相比之下，直流(DC)由电池产生的，只按一个方向流动。

交流发电机二极管整流器转换交直流。这些电子器件可使电流转易地流向一个方向。当电流反转向试图以相反的方向流动时，二极管阻止反流。

大多数交流发电机有六个二极管连接到定子前端接线端子。三个正向二极管允许直流电流从交流发电机的三个绕组流向各种电器配件和电池。三个负二极管让从电池的负极端子流到交流发电机。当然，当电流返回到交流发电机时，电能已在电池及配件做过功了。电流通过搭铁回路流回发电机。

调节器

发电机必须产生一个大电流给电池充电并提供电流让各种电气系统工作。然而，当电池充电完成，发电机必须减少发电量。事实上，如果电流不降低，电池会充电过度。

称为电压调节器的元件调节发电机的发电量，通过改变进入转子绕组或磁场的电流大小实现。如果电池和电器配件得到比他们需要的更多的电流，调节器就减少转子电流。定子上发电就减少。发电机流向电池和电器配件的电流就减少，如电池充电不满或电器用电量比发电机发电量多，调节器增加转子磁场电流，发电机流向电池和电器配件的电流就增加。

一些调节器有电磁开关控制流向转子电路的电流量。正常运行时，这些开关让发电机产生刚好能满足电池和电器配件工作需要的电量。其他类型的稳压器使用晶体管来控制电流流到交流发电机。

发电机调节器类型有：振动继电器电压调节器，晶体管调节器和集成电路调节器。

振动继电器电压调节器

该调节器具有两个重要的部分：(1) 限流电阻；(2) 继电器。

继电器控制交流发电机的转子电流。当你打开点火钥匙启动汽车，电流通过闭合开关从电池流到调节器B(即电池)端。这个电流通过继电器的闭合触点和调节器的F端。从那里，流到交流发电机的F端，从而提供电流到转子。电流进入转子磁场绕组产生磁场，磁场在定子绕组产生电流。定子绕组电流流经二极管至发电机电池端到电池。电池充电时，电池电压增加。增加的电压加强了调节电器继电器的磁场。因此，电磁铁拉下继电器，切断下活动触点和固定触点之间的电路。

电阻丝减小流向转子的电流量。因此，较小的电流回流到电池和电器配件。尽管减少了电流，但电池接受的电流仍然比它需要的多，特别是驾驶员使用的电器不多时。如果太多的电流仍达到电池，电池电压也会太大。在这种情况下，从蓄电池来的高电压流向继电器，拉下上活动触点抵住静触点，这样，上动触点接地。电流只能搭铁。

全晶体管调节器

全晶体管调节器取代振动继电器调节器，因为晶体管继电器没有能够磨损的运动部件。

全晶体管调节器用晶体管控制转子磁场电流。晶体管是可以控制电流微小的电子开关，晶体管在设定的电压工作。例如，你会找到设定值为13.5伏特的调节器。如果电压增加超过此值，晶体管电阻也增加。这会减少电流以满足汽车减少了的电量需求。

如果电压下降至低于13.5伏，晶体管电阻降低。晶体管的电流流动增加，以满足汽车增加的电量需求。

全晶体管调节器的外观像振动继电器调节器。然而，全晶体管外形可能小很多。两种调节器连接相同。通过同样的端子流向和流出调节器至转子绕组。

充电系统的维护

要使交流发电机正常工作，皮带须状态良好、松紧恰当。当你每月定期检查电器，扭一下皮带查看皮带的工作面或底面。如有裂纹或烧灼，尽快更换。

常用的驱动带有超过100个不同的尺寸。如果长途旅行，你应为车子的发电机和冷却泵配备用皮带。即使你不想自己更换皮带，备有皮带也会有用，因为服务站的皮带规格不一定适合你的车。

检查发电机皮带有两个办法。一种方法是按下带轮之间的皮带检查松紧度。如果你能将皮带向下移动超过其静止位置的半英寸，它需要调紧。另一种方法是皮带连接后转动发电机皮带轮，如果你能轻松转动发电机皮带轮，则说明皮带过松。

发电机皮带过松会打滑，发电机速度不能快到足以让电池充电。最终，当发动机加速，皮带表面磨得发亮并发出尖叫。皮带轮打滑产生的热量会烧灼橡胶而使皮带加快开裂和断掉。

另一方面，皮带太紧会损坏组件的轴承，包括发电机和/或水泵。

为了最大可靠性，建议您每三年或36 000公里更换驱动皮带，以先发生者为准。虽然皮带使用时间可以超过三年，定期更换他们可以避免大部分的问题。

Unit 9

Ignition System

扫码获取
扩展视频

There are many different ignition systems. Most of these systems can be placed into one of three distinct: the conventional breaker point type ignition systems (in use since the early 1900s); the electronic ignition systems (popular since the mid 70s); and the distributorless ignition system (introduces in the mid 80s).

The automotive ignition system has two basic functions; it must control the spark and timing of the spark plug firing to match varying engine requirements, and it must increase battery voltage to a point where it will overcome the resistance offered by the spark plug gap and fire the plug.

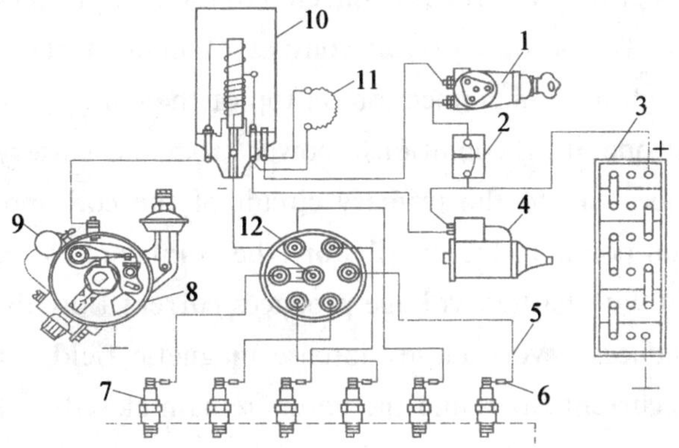

Fig. 9 - 1 point-type ignition system

1. switch 2. amperometer 3. battery 4. startor 5. cable 6. resistance 7. spark plug 8. breaker 9. capacitor 10. coil 11. add-on resistance 12. distributor

Point-Type Ignition System

An automotive ignition system is divided into two electrical circuits—the primary and secondary circuits. The primary circuit carries low voltage. This circuit operates only on battery current and is controlled by the breaker points and the ignition switch. The secondary circuit contains coil (commonly called the coil wire), the distributor cap, the distributor rotor, the spark plug leads and the spark plugs.

The distributor is the controlling element of the system. It switches the primary current on and off and distributes the current to the proper spark plug each time a spark is needed. The distributor is a stationary housing surrounding a rotating shaft. The shaft is driven at one-half engine speed by the engine's camshaft through the distributor drive gears. A cam near the top of the distributor shaft has one lobe for each cylinder of the engine. The cam operates the contact points, which are mounted on a plate within the distributor housing.

A rotor is attached to the top of the distributor shaft. When the distributor cap is in place, a spring-loaded piece of metal in the center of the cap makes contact with a metal strip on top of the rotor. The outer end of the rotor passes very close to the contacts connected to the spark plug leads around the outside of the distributor cap.

The coil is the heart of the ignition system. Essentially, it is nothing more than a transformer which takes the relatively low voltage (12 volts) available from the battery and increasing it to a point where it will fire the plug as much as 40000 volts. The term "coil" is perhaps a misnomer since there are actually two coils of wire wound about an iron cone. These coils are insulated from each other and the whole assembly is enclosed in an oil-filled case. The primary coil, which consists of relatively few turns of heavy wire, is connected to the two primary terminals located on top of the coil. The secondary coil consists of many turns of fine wire. It is connected to the high-tension connection on top of the coil.

Under normal operating conditions, power from the battery is fed through a resistor or resistance wire to the primary circuit of the coil and is then grounded through the ignition points in the distributor (the points are closed). Energizing the coil primary circuit with battery voltage produces current flow through the primary winding, which induces a very large, intense magnetic field. This magnetic field remains as long as current flows and the points remain closed.

As the distributor cam rotates, the points are pushed apart, breaking the primary circuit and stopping the flow of current. Interrupting the flow of primary current causes the magnetic field to collapse. Just as current flowing through a wire produces a magnetic field, moving a magnetic field across a wire will produce a current. As the magnetic field collapses, its lines of wire in the secondary winding, induce a current in them. Since there are many more turns of wire in the secondary windings, the voltage from the primary winding is magnified considerably up to 40 000 volts.

The voltage from the coil secondary winding flows through the coil high-tension lead to the center of the distributor cap, where it is distributed by the rotor to one of the outer terminals in the cap. From there, it flows through the spark plug lead to the spark plug. This process occurs in a split second and is repeated every time the points open and close, which is up to 1 500 times a minute in a 4-cylinder engine at idle.

Electronic Ignition Systems

The need for higher mileage, reduced emissions and greater reliability has led to the development of the electronic ignition system. These system generate a much stronger spark, which is needed to ignite leaner fuel. Breaker point system needed a resistor to reduce the operating voltage of the primary circuit in order to prolong the life of the points. The primary circuit of the electronic ignition system operates on full battery voltage, which helps to develop a stronger spark. Spark plug gaps have winded due to the ability of the increased voltage to jump the large gap. Cleaner combustion and less deposits have led to longer spark plug life.

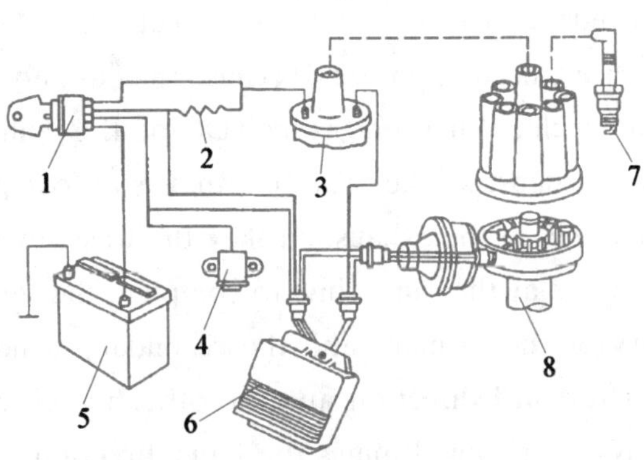

Fig. 9－2 electronic ignition system

1. key 2. resistance 3. ignition coil 4. sensor 5. battery
6. ignition control unit 7. spark plug 8. distributor

On some systems, the ignition coil has moved inside the distributor cap. This system is said to have an internal coil opposed to the complicated external.

Electronic ignition systems are not as complicated as they may first appear. In fact, they differ only slightly from conventional point ignition systems. Like conventional ignition systems, electronic systems have two circuits: a primary circuit and a secondary circuit. The entire secondary circuit is the same as in a conventional ignition system. In addition, the section of the primary circuit from the battery to the battery terminal at the coil is the same as in a conventional ignition system.

Electronic ignition system differ from conventional ignition system in the distributor component area. Instead of a distributor cam, breaker plate, points, and condenser, an electronic ignition system has an armature (called by various names such as a trigger wheel, redactor, etc.), a pickup coil (stator, sensor, etc.), and an electronic module.

Distributorless Ignition System (DIS)

The third type of ignition system is the distributorless ignition. The spark plugs are fired directly from the coils. The spark timing is controlled by an Ignition Control Unit (ICU) and the Engine Control Unit (ECU). The distributorless ignition system may have one coil per cylinder, or one coil for each pair of cylinders.

Some popular systems use one ignition coil per two cylinders. This type of system is often known as the waste spark distribution method. In this system, each cylinder is paired with the cylinder opposite it in the firing order (usually 1-4-2-3 on 4-cylinder engines or 1-4-2-5-3-6 on V6 engines). The ends of each coil secondary leads are attached to spark plugs for the paired opposites. These two plugs are on companion cylinder, cylinders that are at Top Dead Center (TDC) at the same time. But, they are paired opposites, because they are always at opposing ends of the 4-stroke engine cycle. When one is at TDC of the compression stroke, the other is at TDC of the exhaust stroke. The one that is on compression is said to be the event cylinder and one on the exhaust stroke, the waste cylinder. When the coil discharges, both plugs fire at the same time to complete the series circuit.

Since the polarity of the primary and the secondary windings are fixed, one plug always fires in a forward direction and the other in reverse. This is different than a conventional system firing all plugs the same direction each time. Because of the demand for additional energy; the coil design, saturation time and primary current flow are also different. This redesign of the system allows higher energy to be available from the distributorless coils, greater than 40 kilovolts at the rpm ranges.

The distributorless ignition system uses either a magnetic crankshaft sensor, camshaft position sensor, or both, to determine crankshaft position and engine speed. This signal is sent to the ignition control module or engine control module, which then energizes the appropriate coil.

The advantage of no distributor, in theory, is:

1. No timing adjustments.
2. No distributor cap and rotor.
3. No moving parts to wear out.
4. No distributor to accumulate moisture and cause staring problems.
5. No distributor to drive thus providing less engine drag.

The major components of a distributorless ignition are:

1. ECU or Engine Control Unit.

2. ICU or Ignition Control Unit.

3. Magnetic Triggering Device such as the Crankshaft Position Sensor and the Camshaft position Sensor.

4. Coil Pack.

NEW WORDS

distinct	[dɪˈstɪŋkt]	*adj.*	不同的
conventional	[kənˈvenʃənl]	*adj.*	传统的
match	[mætʃ]	*v.*	匹配
voltage	[ˈvəultɪdʒ]	*n.*	电压
gap	[gæp]	*n.*	间隙
secondary	[ˈsekənderi]	*adj.*	次级的
breaker	[ˈbreɪkə]	*n.*	断路器
essentially	[ɪˈsenʃəli]	*adv.*	本质上
misnomer	[ˌmɪsˈnəumə]	*n.*	用错的名字
insulate	[ˈɪnsjuleɪt]	*v.*	隔离
magnetic	[mægˈnetɪk]	*adj.*	磁电式的
interrupt	[ˌɪntəˈrʌpt]	*vt.*	中断
mileage	[ˈmaɪlɪdʒ]	*n.*	里程数
reliability	[rɪˌlaɪəˈbɪlɪti]	*n.*	可靠性
terminal	[ˈtɜːmɪnl]	*n.*	端子
per	[pə]	*prep.*	每，按照
saturation	[ˌsætʃəˈreɪʃn]	*n.*	磁饱和
Turn	[tɜːn]	*n.*	匝数
transformer	[trænsˈfɔːmə(r)]	*n.*	变压器
series	[ˈsɪəriːz]	*n.*	串联
condenser	[kənˈdensə]	*n.*	电容器

PHRASES

conventional breaker point type ignition systems	传统触点式点火系统
distributorless ignition system	无分电器点火系统
timing of the spark plug firing	点火正时
the primary and secondary circuit	初级与次级电路

distributor rotor 分电器轴
distributor cap 分火头
under normal operating conditions 正常运行条件下
firing order 点火次序
magnetic crankshaft sensor 电磁式曲轴传感器

REVIEW QUESTIONS

(1) List the different types of ignition system.

(2) What is the function of the distributor?

(3) What is the difference between electronic ignition system and conventional ignition system?

(4) Please introduce the distributorless ignition system.

(5) What is advantage of no distributor?

REFERENCE TRANSLATION

点火系统

点火系统有多种。这些系统可以分为三类:传统触点式点火系统(20世纪初开始使用);电子点火系统(70年代中期普通开始采用);无分电器点火系统(80年代中期开始使用)。

汽车点火系统有两个基本作用,须能控制点火正时与火花塞点火以满足不同发动机的要求,须能产生足够高的电压以克服火花塞间隙的电阻。

触点式点火系统

汽车点火系统分为两个电路——初级和次级电路。初级电路电压低。该电路由电池供电由触点和点火开关控制。次级电路有线圈(俗称绕组)、分电器盖、分火头、火花塞导线和火花塞。

分电器是系统的控制元件,它开关初级电流并正确分配电流到每个火花塞。分电器是一个包着旋转轴的静止壳体。轴由发动机凸轮驱动分电器齿轮转动,速度为发动机的一半。分电器轴顶部有一个凸轮对应发动机的每个气缸。凸轮操作安装于分电器壳体上的触点。

转子安装在分电器轴的上部,安装好分电器盖后,盖子中心的金属片在弹簧作用下紧贴转子顶部的金属条。转子外端十分贴近地通过触点与分电器盖四周的火花塞分火头接触。

点火线圈是点火系统的心脏。基本上,它只不过是一个变压器,将来自电池的相对较低电压(12伏)增加到达40 000伏特以给火花塞点火。术语“线圈”或许是一个误称,因为实际上有两对线圈缠绕在铁芯上。这些线圈彼此绝缘,整个装置封闭在一个充满油的盒子里。初级线圈匝数少直径粗,连接到位于线圈上方的两个初级端子上。次级线圈由许多的匝数细线组成,它连接到线圈顶部高压端。

在正常运行时,电池电源通过一个电阻或电阻丝线圈接到初级电路,然后通过分配器触点接地(触点关闭)。给初级线圈通电,电池电压产生的电流通过初级绕组,导致一个非常大的强磁场。只要触点闭合,电流流过就有这个磁场。

当分电器凸轮转动时,触点断开,初级电路断开,电流消失。中断初级电流流动导致磁场急剧减弱。就像流过电流的导线产生磁场一样,在磁场运动导线会产生电流。当磁场减弱时,次级绕组上的导线上会产生感应电流。因为有很多匝的次级绕组,初级绕组的电压会放大很多高达 40 000 伏。

次级绕组的电压流过分电器盖中心高压端子,再由转子分配至分电器盖上外围端子,然后它流经火花塞端子到火花塞。这个过程发生在一瞬间,其间触点每打开和关闭一次就重复一次,4 缸发动机怠速时约一分钟 1 500 次。

电子点火系统

对提高使用寿命、减少排放量和提高可靠性的需要,促使电子点火系统的发展。这些系统产生更强的火花,这是点燃稀薄混合气所需要的。触点式点火系统需加一电阻以减小初级电路的工作电压,延长触点生命。而电子点火系统的初级电路在电池满电压下工作,这有助于产生更强大的火花。高电压提高了击穿火花塞间隙的跳火能力。燃烧更清洁,积炭减少,延长了火花塞寿命。

有些系统点火线圈装在分电器盖里,与复杂外置式对应,称为内置线圈。

电子点火系统并不像刚出现时那么复杂。事实上,他们只稍不同于传统的点式点火系统。像传统的点火系统一样,电子系统有两个电路:初级电路和次级电路。整个次级电路与传统点火系统一样。此外,该部分的主电路从电池到电池端子的线圈也与传统点火系统一样。

电子点火系统与传统点火系统的区别在于分配器组件区域。电子点火系统不是由分配器凸轮、断路器板、触点和电容组成,它有一个电枢(有不同称谓如触发器、发生器等)、拾波线圈(定子、传感器等)和一个电子模块。

无分电器点火系统(DIS)

第三类点火系统是无分电器点火。火花塞由线圈直接点火。点火正时由点火控制单元(ICU)和发动机控制单元(ECU)控制。无分电器点火系统可能每缸有一个点火线圈,或每对气缸一个线圈。

大多系统每两缸使用一个点火线圈。这种类型的系统通常称为废火花点火法。在这个系统中,成对气缸以一定点火顺序点火(通常是四缸发动机 1 4 2 3 或 V6 发动机 1 4 2 5 3 6)。每个点火线圈次级导线的两端连接到以上的成对火花塞上。这两个火花塞在成对气缸上,都同时处于上上点(TDC)。但是完全相反,因为他们总是在 4 冲程发动机的相反工作端循环。当一个在压缩行程的上止点,另一个是在排气行程上止点。这样,压缩上止点的一个是正常点火,排气上止点的另一个火花浪费。线圈放电时,两个火花塞同时点火，串联电路完成一个回路。

由于初级和次级绕组的极性是固定的，一个火花塞正向点火一个反向点火。这是不同于传统系统分时同向给火花塞点火。由于额外的能量需求；线圈设计、饱和时间和初级电流也不同。这个重新设计的系统允许无分电器线圈产生更高的能量，在转速范围内高达 40 千伏。

无分电器点火系统装有一个由磁式曲轴传感器或凸轮轴位置传感器或两者都用，来确定曲轴位置和发动机转速。这个信号送至点火控制模块或发动机控制模块，从而使相应的线圈通电。

理论上，无分电器系统的优势是：

1. 无点火正时调整装置。

2. 无分电器盖和转子。

3. 没有运动部件磨损。

4. 没有分电器积聚水分并造成打火问题。

5. 没有分电器驱动所以发动机阻力小。

无分电器点火的主要元件是：

1. ECU 或发动机控制单元。

2. ICU 或点火控制单元。

3. 磁性触发装置，如曲轴位置传感器与凸轮轴位置传感器。

4. 线圈组。

Unit 10

Electronic Fuel Injection System

扫码获取
扩展视频

Automobile engineers are continually striving towards minimal fuel consumption and cleaner exhaust emissions. The application of electronic control, once too complex and expensive, is becoming more and more a remarkably straight-forward economical solution.

Engine power, fuel consumption and exhaust emission all depend on the accuracy of the air-fuel-ratio. With petrol engines there are many operating conditions under which it is difficult to ensure the correct air-fuel ratio will always be delivered to the engine's cylinders for combustion.

When the induced air quantity equals the theoretical air requirements for complete combustion, the equivalence ratio (also known as the excess air ratio) is said to be 100% or equals 1. When the induced air is less than theoretical (rich mixture) the ratio is less than 1; 85 - 95%, or 0.85 - 0.95. When the induced air is more than theoretical (weak or lean mixture) the ratio is more than 1; 102 - 120% or 1.02 - 1.2.

In most cases a narrow band of ratios (0.9 to 1.1) have proved optimal. To keep equivalence ratios within these limits, the actual quantity of air entering the cylinder must be known so that the precise amount of fuel quantity can be supplied.

A carburetor is a mechanical device that is neither totally accurate nor particularly fast in responding to changing engine requirements. Adding electronic feedback mixture control improves a carburetor's fuel metering capabilities under some circumstances, but most of the work is still done mechanically by the many jets, passages, and air bleeds. Adding feedback controls and other emission related devices in recent years has resulted in very complex carburetors that are extremely expensive to repair or replace.

The intake manifold also is a mechanical device that, when teamed with a carburetor, results in less than ideal air-fuel control. Because of a carburetor's limitations, the manifold must locate it centrally over V-engines, or next to inline engines, the intake ports while remaining within the space limitations under the hood. The manifold runners have to be kept as short as possible to minimize fuel delivery lag, and there can not be any low points where fuel might puddle. These restrictions severely limit the amount of manifold tuning possible, and even the best designs still have problems with fuel condensing on cold manifold walls.

The solution to the problem posed by a carbureted fuel system is electronic fuel injection (EFI). EFI provides precise mixture control over all speed ranges and under all operating conditions. Its fuel delivery components are simpler and often less expensive than a feedback carburetor. Some designs allow a wider range of manifold designs. Equally important is that EFI offers the potential of highly reliable electronic control.

Electronic fuel injection (EFI) has made conventional carburetors about as out of date as the Model T. All fuel systems can be broken down to three subsystems:

1. Fuel-supply system: Includes the fuel pump, lines, and filters that feed clean fuel to the fuel metering system.

2. Fuel metering system: Includes all parts that control the correct amount of fuel entering the engine.

3. Air-intake system: Includes air filters, ducts and valves that control how much clean air enters the engine.

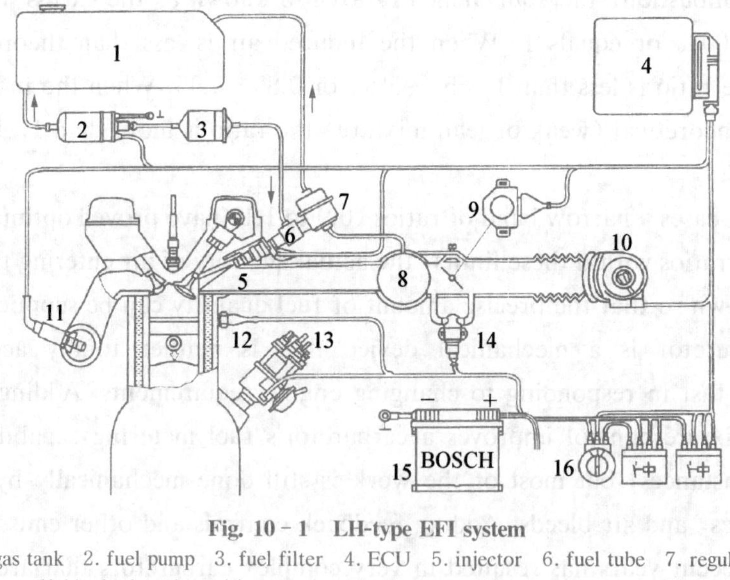

Fig. 10 - 1 LH-type EFI system

1. gas tank 2. fuel pump 3. fuel filter 4. ECU 5. injector 6. fuel tube 7. regulator 8. manifold 9. throttle position sensor 10. air meter 11. oxygen sensor 12. coolant temperature sensor 13. distributor 14. idle air valve 15. battery 16. ignition switch

Electronic fuel injection, like carburetion, is a way of delivering the correct air/fuel mixture to the engine at the correct time under different operating conditions. Electronic fuel injection, however, is much simpler, more precise, and more reliable because it is controlled electronically rather than mechanically. In an EFI system microprocessor controlled fuel injectors supply the engine with the optimum amount of fuel under all driving conditions. To this end fast acting microprocessors can recalculate an engine's fuel needs 167 times per second.

With EFI a microprocessor receives electrical signals from various sensors, supplying data about air induction volume or mass, engine speed, coolant and air temperature, and throttle position. This information is used to determine the optimum air-fuel mixture for the demands being placed on the engine.

There are three methods of regulating the quantity of fuel injected:

1. Continuous injection: where the quantity can be regulated by varying the fuel pressure.

2. Intermittent injection: where the fuel pressure is constant and the quantity and the quantity regulated by the time-period during which the injectors are delivering fuel with phased injection relative to the opening of the inlet valve.

3. Intermittent injection without times or phased injection relative to the opening of the inlet valve.

Coupled with these methods, it is possible to have systems using only one injector per engine (single point fuel injection or throttle body injection (TBI) or one injector per cylinder (multipoint fuel injection or port fuel injection).

In port fuel injection systems, a solenoid fuel injector uses a coil and close the needle valve. When energized by the computer, the coil's magnetic field attracts the armature and needle valve. This pulls the needle valve open and fuel sprays out of the nozzle. A spring pushes the injector needle valve closed when no signal is sent to the coil winding.

Fuel filters provide extremely fine filtration to protect the small metering orifices in the injector nozzles. The nozzles can not normally be easily cleaned; if they become clogged, the injector may have to be replaced. For this reason, filter replacement at recommended intervals is critical. Also, fuel pumps and pressure regulators are usually highly reliable factory sealed units not meant to be adjusted or overhauled but, instead, replaced.

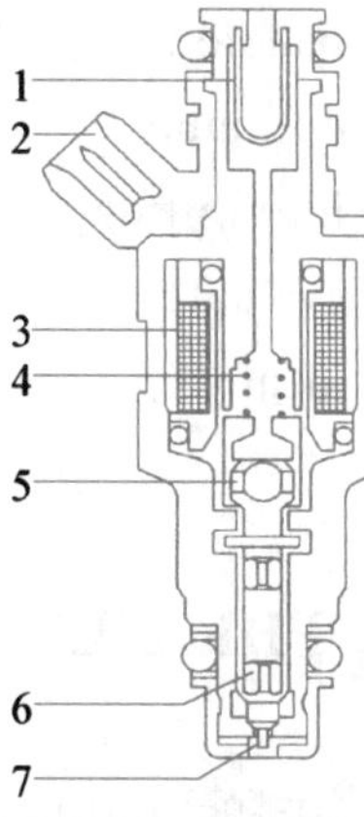

Fig. 10 - 2 fuel injector
1. filter 2. electric plug
3. magnetic coil 4. spring
5. armature 6. needle valve
7. noozle

TBI utilizes a central fuel-mixing feature similar to a carburetor along with an electronically controlled injector valve. Some TBI systems use only one injector (smaller engines), while two injectors are required for larger, more powerful V-6 and V-8 engines. The injector or injectors, located inside what amounts to a carburetor body, sprays the fuel, on command, into an essentially conventional intake manifold. The advantage of TBI over a conventional carburetor is the elimination of a float system, idle, acceleration, and main metering systems, and the choke assembly; these systems are replaced with accurate fuel metering through the injector. Just as throttle body injection improved fuel delivery compared with a carburetor, port injection improved throttle body delivery by metering fuel directly to each cylinder, reducing problems caused by intake manifold shape.

The injector on-time or pulse width, is the length of time (measured in milliseconds) that the injector sprays fuel or stays open. The on-time of an injector is determined by the microcomputer. A microcomputer receives electrical signals from sensors that monitor different operating conditions. It evaluates the sensor information and, based on this, signals the fuel injector, thereby controlling their ON and OFF pulses. On-time of an injector is increased wide-open throttle. During idle speed and steady throttle (cruise) with a warm engine, on-time is reduced.

NEW WORDS

strive	[straɪv]	*v*.	努力
induce	[in'djuːs]	*v*.	引诱
equivalence	[ɪ'kwɪvələns]	*n*.	等值物
theoretical	[ˌθɪə'retɪkl]	*adj*.	理论上的
lag	[læg]	*v*.	落后
puddle	['pʌdl]	*vt*.	搅拌
optimum	['ɒptɪməm]	*adj*.	最优的
intermittent	[ˌɪntə'mɪtənt]	*adj*.	间歇的
evaluate	[ɪ'væljueɪt]	*vt*.	评估
ideal	[aɪ'diːəl]	*adj*.	理想的

PHRASES

air-fuel ratio	空燃比
excess air ratio	过量空气系数
rich mixture	浓混合气
lean mixture	稀混合气

intake manifold 进气歧管
fuel-metering system 燃油计量系统
single point fuel injection 单点喷射

REVIEW QUESTIONS

(1) Why was the EFI system induced to replace the carburetor?
(2) Explain the concept of air excess ratio to us.
(3) Why is carburetor with feedback also out of date?
(4) What are the EFI's advantages over carburetor system?
(5) What 's the difference between TBI and multipoint injection?

REFERENCE TRANSLATION

电子燃油喷射系统

汽车工程师一直在朝着最小的燃油消耗和更干净的尾气排放而努力，电子控制技术的应用，曾经十分复杂和昂贵，正越来越变成解决燃油经济性的直接方案。

发动机动力、燃油消耗和尾气排放都取决于空燃比的准确度。汽油机的工况复杂，很难确保总是保持正确的空燃比混合气进入气缸燃烧。

当进气量等于理论上完全燃烧的空气量，其等量空燃比（也称过量空气系数）是100%或1，如进气量少于理论值（浓混合气），空燃比小于1，通常是0.81—0.95，如进气量多于理论值（稀混合气），空燃比大于1，一般在1.02—1.2。

在大多情况下，处于0.9到1.1这样狭窄区域的空燃比证明是最佳的。保持空气在这个界限内的空燃比，必须知道实际进入气缸的空气以便于进行供应燃油的精确控制。

化油器是机械装置，计量既不完全准确，对发动机需求的响应也不快速。在有些情况下，增加电子反馈混合气控制提高化油器燃油计量能力，但大多数功能仍是油孔、油道、空气计量孔等机械装置完成。近年来，增加反馈控制和其他尾气排放相关装置已导致化油器十分复杂，以致修理与更换都特别昂贵。

进气歧管也是机械装置，与化油器组合使用会导致达不到理论空燃比控制。因化油器的局限性，进气歧管需装在V发动机中间，直列发动机的前端，进气口也因发动舱空间限制，进气通道不得不尽可能短，最大程度缩小燃油供给滞后，燃油搅拌处不能有任何低点。这些局限性严重限制了进气歧管的优化设计，即使是最优的设计也仍然存在油气冷凝在歧管壁的问题。

解决化油器燃油系统呈现的问题方案是电子燃油喷射系统（EFI），EFI可在所有速度和工况下提供精确的混合气控制，其燃油供给元件更加简单，通常比反馈式化油器还便宜，有些对进气歧管设计形式要求也不严格，同样重要的是，EFI具有高可靠性电子控制的潜力。

EFI 已使传统化油器像 T 型车一样被淘汰。所有的燃油系统可分为三个子系统：

1. 燃油供给系统：包括油泵、油管和提供干净燃油到燃油计量系统的过滤器。

2. 燃油计量系统：包括控制进入发动机油量的所有元件。

3. 进气系统：包括空气过滤器、管道和控制进入发动机干净空气量的气门。

EFI 与化油器一样是在不同工况下在正确时间供给发动机正确空燃混合气的途径，但燃油喷射系统相当简单，更加精确，更加可靠，因它是电子控制而不是机械控制的。在 EFI 系统，微处理器在所有工况下控制发动机最佳燃油供应量。到 20 世纪末，快速微处理器可以每秒计算发动机燃油量需求 167 次。

EFI 的微处理器接受来自各种传感器的电子信号，提供如进气量、发动机速度、冷却液温度和节气门位置等数据，这些信息用于确定发动机需要的最佳空燃比。

调节喷油量有三种方法：

1. 连续喷射：通过调节燃油压力控制油量。

2. 间隙喷射：压力不变，通过调节供油时间长短控制油量，与气门打开时间对应，控制喷油相位。

3. 与气门打开相位无关的间隙喷射。

与这些方法相对应，系统有可能采用每个发动机一个喷油器(单点喷射或节气门体喷射 TBI)，或每个缸一个喷射器(多点喷射或进气口喷射)。

在多点喷射系统，电磁阀用线圈开关喷油针阀，由电脑供电后，线圈磁场吸引电枢和针阀，拉开针阀燃油从喷嘴喷出，没有电信号给线圈绕组时，弹簧复位关闭喷油器针阀。

燃油过滤器提供特别好的过滤作用，保护喷嘴微小的计量孔。一般喷嘴不易清洗，如堵塞必须更换喷油器，因此，定期更换过滤器很重要。同样，油泵和压力调节器通过可靠性很高，由制造厂铅封，不得自行调整，只能更换。

TBI 采用集中燃气混合方式，如同带有电子控制喷油阀的化油器。有些 TBI 系统只有一个喷油器(小型发动机)，大型发动机如 V6 和 V8 采用两个喷油器，喷油器装在节气门体里面，按照指令喷油给本质上很传统式的进气歧管，TBI 比传统化油器的优势是取消了浮子、怠速、加速和主计量系统及喉管组件，这些系统被精确的喷油器燃油计量所取代，就如节气门体喷射比化油器提高燃油供给精度一样，气门口喷射比节气门体喷射精度高，其直接计量喷入每个缸的油量，减少了进气歧管形状带来的问题。

喷油器打开时间或脉冲宽度是喷油器喷射燃油保持打开的时间长度(以微秒计)，喷油时间取决于微处理器，微处理器接收来自监控各种工况的传感器电信号并处理传感器信息，据此发信号给喷油器，控制其 ON 和 OFF 脉冲，节气门打开幅度大，喷油时间增加，暖机后的发动机在怠速时和节气门开度不变(巡航)时，喷油时间减少。

Unit 11

Hybrid Power Cars

扫码获取
扩展视频

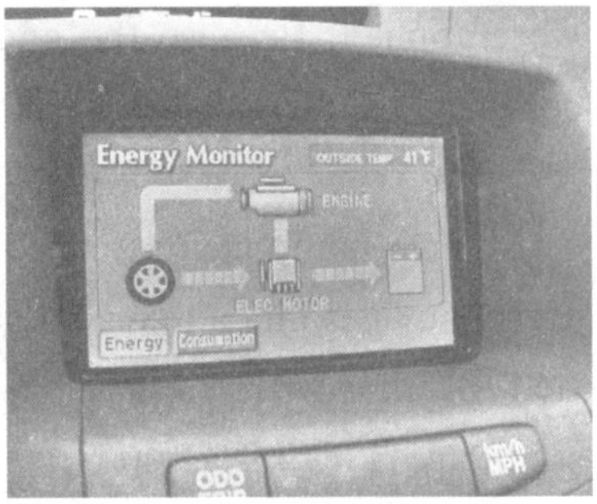

Fig. 11 - 1　energy monitor

The only currently available technology that could meet the zero emissions goal was an electric car. But few people wanted to bear the inconvenience of a car with a range of less than 100 miles, after which they had to plug it into an outlet for hours of recharging.

There is a partial answer to this conundrum available today in the form of an innovative technology that uses existing fuel supplies more efficiently. This promising technology combines a gasoline engine with an electric motor to stretch a gallon of gas further than ever before possible. The vehicles that use this technology are called Hybrids because they use a combination of a very efficient gasoline engine and a hi-tech electric motor to propel the vehicle.

The Concept: How the Hybrid System Works in Simple Terms

Despite the fact that they use electric motors that draw their power from a battery, hybrid vehicles do not have to be plugged in to recharge. The battery is recharged from two sources, and herein lies this system's advantage. The first source is from a generator powered by the internal combustion engine. The second source is through reclaiming the energy that is normally wasted slowing and stopping the vehicle. Let's look at the second method first because that is the most intriguing.

Many of us complain about how much it costs to heat a house, but here we are throwing all of our braking energy to the wind. What if we could capture some of that energy and use it later on to propel the vehicle? Well, that is exactly what a hybrid vehicle does. It uses a property that is inherent in all electric motors: the fact that electric motors and generators are exactly the same. If you send electricity through wires into a motor, it will cause the shaft of the motor to turn, but if you find another way to turn the shaft of an electric motor, it will generate electricity back through those wires.

The more work that a motor has to perform, the more electricity it requires. In the same way, the more electrical power you demand of a generator, the harder it is to turn the shaft. So, if we set the system up so that when you first step on the brakes, it connects this motor/generator to the battery in order to charge it, the effect will be to slow the vehicle down and, voila, we have free energy that we just stored in the battery to be used later to propel the car.

On the other side of the equation, the gasoline engine can be smaller because, when it needs extra power, the electric motor is there to assist in the acceleration using the free energy in the battery that was captured the last time that the brakes were applied. Because the engine doesn't have to be as powerful, it can be more compact and deliver much better gas mileage.

The Prius

Three components make up the power train of the Prius, a 4 cylinder high efficiency gasoline engine, a generator and an electric motor. These components are tied together with a single planetary gear set. There is no transmission beyond that simple gear arrangement.

To start the Prius, you turn the ignition switch to the start position, just like a normal car, but you don't hear anything. Did the car start? The indicators on the graphical display panel say that the car is running, but there is silence. Ok, on a leap of faith you put the Selector Lever in Drive and step on the accelerator pedal and, sure enough, the car takes off silently as though a large invisible hand is pushing you from behind. As you reach about 15 mph, you notice that the gasoline engine is running though you did not hear it start.

Fig. 11 - 2 first mass production hybrid model

During normal cruising above 15 mph, the gasoline engine is doing most of the work while the generator tops off the charge in the battery. Whenever you release the throttle or step on the brake, the electric motor doubles as a generator and charges the battery through regenerative braking. If more power is needed for accelerating or climbing a hill, the electric motor immediately kicks in to assist the gasoline engine using the energy that is stored in the battery. As you slow down and come to a stop, you realize that the gasoline engine is no longer running and the car is dead quiet, an eerie feeling that would have you breaking out into a cold sweat in an ordinary car.

Another thing that you notice as you accelerate is that this car does not shift. The planetary gear set acts as an infinitely variable transmission that gradually transitions from low gear to high gear in a smooth steady flow. The effect is that, while the car picks up speed, the engine seems to stay at its most efficient rpm.

Backing up is handled completely by the electric motor which serves to simplify the system and eliminate the need for a reverse gear.

The Toyota Prius is an environmentally friendly family sedan, that is quite pleasant to drive and easy to live with. Acceleration is a bit leisurely for some of the more aggressive drivers that I know, but it is competent and will handle most traffic situations without a problem.

Fig. 11 - 3 Honda insight picture

The brake feel takes a bit of getting used to. The car stops well, but the brake pedal feel is unusual. On a normal car, the harder that you press on the brake pedal, the stronger the stopping action, but on the Prius, a light pressure on the brake will start with a light braking action that increases in severity even though pedal pressure hasn't changed. I'm not saying that this a safety issue at all.You will adapt to it after a while and learn to compensate until you barely notice it.

The Insight

The Honda Insight is a small two seat commuter car that gets great gas mileage and is a blast to drive and be seen in. It weighs in at a featherweight 1,887 pounds due to a lightweight aluminum body and frame that is 47-percent lighter than an equivalent steel body. Powering the Insight is a 1.0 liter, 3-cylinder VTEC engine coupled to an ultra-thin electric motor that is mounted between the engine and the transmission. The electric motor provides additional power to help the engine when it's needed during acceleration. When slowing down, the motor does double duty as a generator to recharge the battery pack. This "regenerative braking" captures energy that is normally lost through the brakes and stores it in the battery for later use to help propel the car.

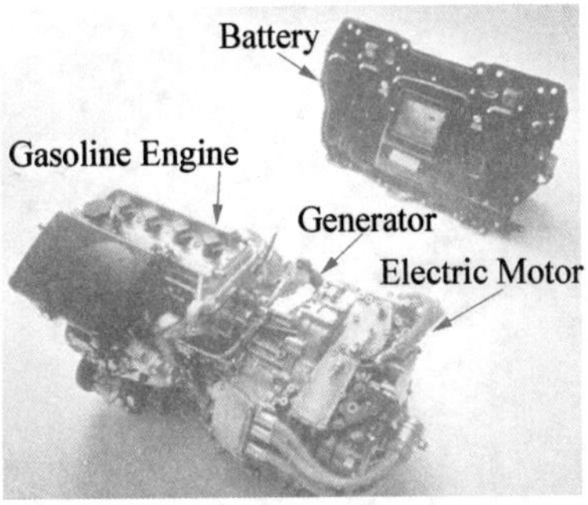

Fig. 11 - 4 main components of hybrid

Unlike the Prius, the Insight has a transmission, either a 5-speed manual or, for 2002, a new CVT automatic, and drives like a normal economy car. The engine is always running when the vehicle is moving, but will sometimes shut itself off when you stop in order to conserve fuel. As soon as you depress the clutch, the engine instantly restarts. The single electric motor is used as an assist to the 3 cylinder gasoline engine, which is the primary source of power. The electric motor becomes a generator when the computer calls upon it to charge the battery.

This system is elegant in its simplicity and certainly delivers the goods with an EPA rating of 61 mpg city and 68 mpg highway for the standard transmission model. These figures earn the Insight top billing as the most fuel efficient car sold in America. The CVT Equipped Insight comes in at a respectable 57 mpg city and 56 mpg highway.

Despite the great gas mileage, this car has good acceleration and is as much fun to drive on winding country roads as it is to dart around in city traffic.

There is only room in this car for two people and their bare essentials since there is very little storage space. As is typical for Honda, the handling and steering feel are excellent. The ride is another story, however. You will feel all the bumps and irregularities of the road surface as you drive this featherweight. Part of the reason for the choppy ride is the small, high-pressure tires that are tailored for the lowest rolling resistance possible.

NEW WORDS

emission	[ɪˈmɪʃn]	*n*.	排放
conundrum	[kəˈnʌndrəm]	*n*.	难题
herein	[ˌhɪərˈɪn]	*adv*.	在这里
equation	[ɪˈkweɪʒn]	*n*.	方程式
throttle	[ˈθrɒtl]	*v*.	节气门
eerie	[ˈɪəri]	*adj*.	奇怪的
shift	[ʃɪft]	*vi*.	换挡
planetary	[ˈplænətri]	*adj*.	行星的
tailor	[ˈteɪlə]	*n*.	裁缝
transition	[trænˈzɪʃn]	*n*.	转变

PHRASES

kick in	开始
low gear	低速挡
power train	传动系

REVIEW QUESTIONS

(1) What's the main difficult problem to overcome for a pure electrical car?
(2) Why is the hybrid auto an effective way to save fuel?
(3) Tell us the power resource change process of a hybrid car for start to stop.
(4) What are the advantages of hybrid car compared to traditional ones?

REFERENCE TRANSLATION

混合动力汽车

现在技术唯一可以满足零排放的是电动汽车技术，但很少有人愿意忍受开不到100英里就需插电接头充电几小时这样的不方便。

现在解决这个问题的一个折中的方法是使燃油效率更高的一个创新性技术，这项富有前景的技术结合汽油机与电动机技术，使单位汽油里程比以前所有的方法更长，使用这种技术的汽车称为混合动力车，因为其使用非常高效的汽油发动机与高技术电动机结合驱动汽车。

概念：简述混合动力系统工作原理

除了也使用取自蓄电池电能的电动机外，混合动力汽车不用插电充电，蓄电池充电有两个方式，正由此显示了混合动力系统的优点，一是由内燃机驱动的发动机供电，二是通过回收减速和停车过程消耗的能量，让我们先看下第二种方法，因其更令人感兴趣。

我们很多人抱怨房子供暖要花很多钱，但刹车时我们却将能量浪费在风中，要是可以回收这些能量驱动汽车是多好的事啊！对了，这正是混合动力所要做的。它利用电动机与发电机本质是一样的特征，如经电机绕组给电机通电，轴会转动，但如用其他的办法转动电机轴，在绕组中就会产生电流。

电机做功越多，需要的电能就越多，同样，发电机发电越多，转动轴的力量就需要越大。所以，如当刚制动时设置系统，电动机/发电机与蓄电池连接充电，结果使汽车减速，也就是我们使能量贮存到蓄电池以后用于驱动汽车。

在这个等式的另一边，汽油机可以做得更小，因其需要额外动力时电动机辅助加速，利用上次刹车回收的电池多余能量，也因发动机不再需功率强大，就可以做得更紧凑，运行寿命更长。

普锐仕

普锐仕传动系统由三个部件组成：四缸高效汽油机、发电机和电动机，这些部件经一个简单的行星齿轮装置连接起来，除此之外，没有别的变速器。

启动普锐仕时，如一般汽车一样转动点火钥匙到启动位置，但你听不到任何声音，汽车启动了吗？图形显示面板指示器显示汽车在运行，但很安静，好，你自信地将换挡杆置于驱动挡，踏下加速踏板，十分确定，汽车会静静地开出，像有无形的大手从后面推着你走。当速度达到15英里每小时，你会注意到发动机工作了，虽然你并没有听到它启动的声音。

15英里以上巡航时，汽油机做功占绝大多数，发电机给电池充满电，只要你松油门踩刹车，电动机就也起发电机作用，通过刹车发电给电池充电，如加速或爬坡需更大能力，电动机立即利用储在电池的电能开始辅助发动机。在减速停车时，你会发现汽油机不再运行，汽车十分安静，开习惯普通汽车的人会突然有一种很奇怪的感觉。

另一件事你也会注意，即到加速时，汽车并不换挡，行星齿轮装置如同无级变速器一样渐渐从低挡切到高挡，十分平顺。最终效果就是汽车加减速，发动机似乎一直工作在最经济转速工况。

倒车完全由电动机控制以简化系统，取消了倒挡齿轮。

丰田普锐仕是个环保型家用车，驾驶舒适，操作方便，对喜爱开快车的人来说加速感觉好，而且对付大多数交通状况处理自如。

刹车感觉呢，稍有不同，需要花一点时间适应，汽车停车没问题，但踏板感觉不寻常，常规汽车上，踏板踩得越重，停车效果越明显，但普锐仕，尽管踩刹车的力量不变，只需轻点刹车，刹车作用由轻快速到重，我并不是说这是个安全问题，你会很快适应它直到感觉不到不同。

Insight

本田Insight是小型两座交通车，续行时程长，驾驶如风，因用轻质铝身车架，轻量型只有1 887磅，比同等钢结构车轻47%。给Insight提供动力的是1.0 L的3缸VTEC发动机加安装在发动机与变速器之间的超薄型电动机，加速时电动机提供额外动力帮助发动机，减速时，电动机也起发电机作用给蓄电池组充电，这种“发电型刹车”回收刹车时通常是将浪费的能量储蓄在蓄电池里，以备驱动汽车之用。

与普锐仕不同，Insight有变速器，5速手动或2002款新型CVT自动变速器，驾驶如同一般经济型车。汽车运行时发动机一直运转，但当你为省油而停车时有时也会熄火，只要踩下离合器发动机立即重新启动，单独的电动机只是作为3缸发动机的助手，发动机才是主动力源，电脑让电动机给电池充电时，电动机就变成了发电机。

这个系统简洁优雅，当仁不让地获得EPA手动变速箱城市61 mpg和公路68 mpg油耗的不俗成绩，Insight的这些特点使它在美国赢得最佳经济型车销量，无级变速技术使之城市燃油消耗为每加仑57英里，公路上为56。

除续行里程大外，这种车加速性能好，不论在城里飞奔还是在弯曲乡村路上行驶都很有乐趣。

因储备箱空间很小，所以只能坐两个人携带必备的一些东西，作为本田一款经典车型，操作和转向感觉非常好，但平稳性却是另一回事了，你会感觉到路面的起起伏伏，这种颠簸的驾驶感部分原因是车型小和为求滚动摩擦最小化设计的高压胎有关。

Unit 12

Vehicle Recovery

扫码获取
扩展视频

Vehicle recovery is the recovery of any vehicle to another place, generally speaking, with a commercial vehicle known as a recovery vehicle, tow truck or spectacle lift.

General Recovery

There are many types of organisations that carry out the recovery of disabled vehicles; however, they can be divided into two distinct areas: Recovery Operators (who undertake the recovery) and Motoring Organisations.

Motoring organisations—or as they are often known, "The Clubs"—are organisations to which the vehicle's driver will belong. They may have made a conscious effort to do this, or they may have got the membership with their new vehicle, through a company scheme, or purchased with an insurance policy.

Fig. 12－1 ask for vehicle recovery

In the event that a member of the public does not have a "club" membership, the police or Highways Agency can arrange recovery of the vehicle at what is called an "Owner's Request" and they will arrange for help to attend.

Recovery operators are the people who undertake the recovery. They are known by different names around the world, including "patrols," "tow men" and "wrecker drivers". Some are the people used by the motoring organisations to rescue their members. A small percentage will be on the payroll of the motoring organisation and will work exclusively for them. Examples are the patrols used by the AA, RAC and Mondial in the UK. Most recovery operators, however, work for privately owned companies or are individuals. They can do large volumes of work for some of the motoring organisations, but they will normally also do work for the public. In Europe, the percentage of this "private" work is low due to the high profiles of the motoring organisations. Of course some will never do work for the motoring organisations, preferring to work just for their own customers. In the USA, motoring organisations are still growing.

Although there have always been auto repair shops and garages who towed or recovered any vehicles, it is only really in the last fifty years that vehicle recovery has become an industry distinct from the auto repair trade.

A Brief History of the Industry in the UK

Early motorists were often capable of carrying out minor repairs themselves, but as automobiles become more complicated, this become more difficult to carry out successfully. Some early local motoring clubs tried to support their members by encouraging them to help each other. A rota of members who would help other members was kept and in some cases, cash was put aside to hire a tow vehicle if needed.

By the start of the 20th century, some motoring clubs had become large enough to offer roadside assistance service. In the UK, they were The Automobile Association (formed in 1905) and the Royal Automobile Club (formed in 1897 and named Royal in 1907). The services offered were limited to repairs if possible, if not a tow to local garage or the driver's home if nearby (in all cases a limit of 20 miles). During the 1950s, both clubs installed radios to allow them to dispatch patrols straight to the incident. Prior to this, the patrols had needed to go to a patrol box and "phone in" to see if there were any jobs available.

In 1969 and 1970, a number of Midland based recovery clubs were formed and started to offer a "get you home service" from anywhere in the UK. The largest of these was National Breakdown Recovery Club (today known as Green Flag), who also offered to cover you if you had an accident, something almost unheard of up until then.

Unlike the AA and RAC, these new clubs did not operate patrols or have their own recovery vehicles. Instead, they recruited recovery operators to work as their agents. These agents were selected from the best garages and coachworks. Inspections of the equipment and facilities were regularly carried out, by the clubs' own inspectors.

Fig. 12 - 2 lift tow

Within a few years the AA and then the RAC responded with their own get you home or relay services.

Recovery Equipment

Soft Tow

Used for very short distances where a rope, chain, or a length of webbing is attached to the casualty, which must have a working braking system as it will be used to slow both vehicles. This can be dangerous, unless both drivers are competent enough to do it. Although many people believe this is illegal on motorways it is not in Europe, as long as the relevant trailer laws are complied with, i.e., correctly configured lights and signing, observing trailer speed limits, etc.

Rigid (or Bar) Tow

Used for very short distances where a solid metal bar is attached to the casualty. Used mainly with commercial vehicles, which often have a towing eye in the front bumper. In the case of cars and light vans, the towing vehicle can be used for braking, if the bar is kept straight. With commercial vehicles, it is common to connect an air feed to the casualty to allow the tow vehicle's brakes to also operate the casualty's brakes.

Lift Tow (Suspend Tow Crane)

Chains were attached, usually around the casualty's suspension, and some form of packing (often a seat squab or tyre) was inserted between the lifting frame and the casualty. This frame was lifted by means of a pulley until the casualty's wheels were clear of the ground.

Lift Tow (Underlift)

The lift tow is the most common modern method for short distance transportation. The casualty is winched onto a lifting grid and then raised by lifting the grid, with the casualty's tires strapped to the grid. It is more common to use a set of lifting forks to attach to the suspension, axle or chassis of the casualty.

Transportation (Total Lift)

The preferred way to travel any distance. Some transporter designs are very sophisticated, with bodes that "demount" to give a low loading angle. There are also transporters with totally enclosed bodies, used for example for the transportation of prestige vehicles, or vehicles involved in crime that are going for forensic analyses.

Variations of the Above

They were designed to be towed behind a suitable towing vehicle. Another portable device was a crane, which clipped on to an articulated tractor unit's fifth wheel coupling. Total lift dollies were carried by some spectacle lifts to place under the wheels at the opposite end to the lifted wheels, thereby converting the half lift into a total lift. These are used, for example, when a vehicle has had an accident and both ends are damaged.

Other Equipment

Modern recovery vehicles include power units to supply air for power tools or pumping off vehicle breaking systems, etc. Generators supply 110 or 220 volt mains

Fig. 12-3 service equipment

power for floodlighting, tools, etc. There are different shaped forks for attaching to lift points, or for modifying standard lifting devices to allow them to transport motorbikes.

Some recovery vehicles are equipped as mobile workshops or service vans. They will carry a large selection of tools, spares and garage equipment, such as jacks and vehicle stands. In recent years many have also been equipped with spectacle lifts that fold away inside the rear doors.

Communications

In the early days of vehicle recovery, the driver of an automobile would have to contact his or her club or local garage in some way when it failed. Telephones were supplied for this purpose by some motoring organisations, and eventually the agencies responsible for the major roads networks would install them on some hard shoulders. Club patrols would also use the club's phone to check in for work, or wait at their depot for the calls to come in. In the fifties as mobile radios became more reliable, most clubs and some garages fitted them to their vehicles. This had a dramatic effect on ETAs as it was now often possible to divert a returning recovery vehicle before it got back.

To achieve the best use of their assets, all motoring organisations have invested heavily in information technology. Computer software is used to distribute work based on criteria such as nearest vehicle, right equipment (or spares) carried, and of course driver hours regulations. The vehicles are usually fitted with GPS tracking devices, which transmit the vehicle's current location. Motoring organisation vehicles are also fitted with a Mobile Data Terminal, allowing job details to be sent direct to the driver.

Most recovery operators have also invested in IT. Most have job logging software and many have installed in-vehicle communication devices and GPS tracking devices. The distribution of work to the fleet is a very skilful job and the person doing it is often under intense strain. They are known as dispatchers in the USA and controllers in the UK. Because operators are expected to take calls 24 hours a day, some smaller ones pass their telephones to message services after hours.

NEW WORDS

criteria	[kraɪ'tɪərɪə]	*n.*	标准
forensic	[fə'rensɪk]	*n.*	司法鉴定
winch	[wɪntʃ]	*n.*	绞车
suspension	[sə'spenʃn]	*n.*	悬架
casualty	['kæʒuəlti]	*n.*	伤亡人员;事故车
relevant	['reləvənt]	*adj.*	有关的
webbing	['webɪŋ]	*n.*	带子
dispatch	[dɪ'spætʃ]	*vt.*	调度
minor	['maɪnə(r)]	*adj.*	少量的
wrecker	['rekə(r)]	*n.*	救援清障
patrol	[pə'trəʊl]	*vt.*	巡逻
club	[klʌb]	*n.*	会员
conscious	['kɒnʃəs]	*adj.*	有意识的
organisation	[ˌɔːgənaɪ'zeɪʃn]	*n.*	组织
distinct	[dɪ'stɪŋkt]	*adj.*	不同的

PHRASES

vehicle recovery	汽车救援
disabled vehicles	抛锚汽车
insurance policy	保险单

REFERENCE TRANSLATION

汽车救援

汽车救援需将汽车拖到另一个地方,一般由商业性用车如救援车、拖车、举升机实施。

一般性救援

有很多类型的组织承担抛锚汽车救援,但他们分成两个不同的部分:救援实施者(具体承担救援任务)和机动车组织。

机动车组织即我们熟知的俱乐部,由驾驶员参与,或者做很多工作,或者按公司流程与汽车一起加入为会员，或购买保险。

对于非俱乐部会员，警察或高速部门按车主请求可安排予以救援。

救援实施者是承担救援的人，世界各国对其称呼不同，像“patrols，”“tow men”和“wrecker drivers”，有些人是机动车组织成员对会员进行救援，少部分人是机动车组织雇佣专门用于救援，比如英国的 AA，RAC 和 Mondial，但大多数救援人是为私人企业或个人工作，他们为驾驶员协会做了大量工作，但也会为普通百姓服务，在欧洲，为个人服务比例较低，因参加协会的驾驶员比例较高。当然，有些人宁愿为他们自己的顾客服务也从不会为组织服务。在美国，这些组织的数量仍在增加。

虽然已有汽车修理厂可以拖车救援，也仅在五十年前道路救援才从汽车修理业务中脱离开来成为单独的一个行业。

英国汽车救援简述

早期的驾驶员自己能够进行一些简单的汽车维修，但随着汽车越来越复杂，自己修理汽车变得越来越难。一些早期地方性汽车俱乐部试图支援会员互相帮助，一些愿意提供帮助的会员坚持了下来，但有时需要额外花钱租拖车。

20 世纪初，一些俱乐部已经很大，足够提供路边维修服务。在英国，有成立于 1905 年的汽车协会和成立于 1897 年 1907 年被命名为“皇家”的皇家汽车俱乐部，它们的服务限定在可能范围内的维修，且不用拖车即可到修理厂或驾驶员家里，且不是很远(一般在 20 英里内)。20 世纪五十年代中期，两个俱乐部都安装了无线电，用来直接调度队员到事故现场，在此之前，巡逻队员需要到巡逻站点打电话至站点问是否有救援工作要做。

1969—1970 年，一些内陆救援俱乐部成立起来，开始在英国提供任意地方的到家服务，其中最大的一家是英国抛锚车救援俱乐部(现在叫绿旗)，如你发生事故，他们提供帮助涉及当时闻所未闻的内容。

与 AA 和 RAC 不同，这些新型俱乐部不巡逻也没有自己的救援车，他们作为代理机构招募工作人员，代理是从最好的修理厂中选择而来。由俱乐部自己的检查员定期检查装备设施。

仅几年间，AA 和 RAC 也参与服务到家和中介服务。

救援设备

软拖

用于很短的短途，用绳子、链条装在涉事车上，需有刹车系统给两车减速，这样做有点危险，除非两个驾驶员都足够胜任。尽管许多人认为在公路上这样做是非法的，但在欧洲没关系，只要相关拖车法规中编写有如正确确认灯光标志、观察拖车速度限制等。

硬拖

用于很短的短途，用金属棒连接到涉事车上，主要用于商业汽车，常用前保险杠上装有拖车孔。对小轿车和小货车，拖车杆处于直线时可用作刹车；对商务车，常将拖车压缩空气接到事故车上来操作事故车的刹车系统。

举升拖(悬挂拖柄)

常由链条将事故车悬架连起来,用各种形状的东西塞入举升机与事故车之间(常是坐垫或轮胎),用滑轮拉起车架直到事故车车轮完全离开地面。

举升拖(上举式)

举升拖是现代短距离运输常用的方法,涉事车装在举升机举升架上再升起举升架,事故车轮胎限制在架子里,较常用的是一组举升叉抵住悬架、前后桥或汽车底盘。

运输(全举升式)

全举升式对任何距离都是最佳方法,有些运输车设计十分精巧,车身设计成减轻拖车负载的角度,有些运输车为全封闭式,用于运输贵重车辆或涉及犯罪准备用于证据分析的车辆。

变形拖车

这种装置设计成适合安装于拖车的后部,另一个便携式装置是起重臂,以关节形式折叠在拖拉机后的五轮装置上,举升台架装于双柱举升机之上,双柱位于左右相对称的车轮之下用以举起车轮,这样就把半举升变成全举升。这种用在比如当汽车发生事故前后部位都受损的情况。

其他设备

现代救援汽车包括动力单元供应空气给动力工具或供气给汽车刹车系统等,发电机供电 110 V 或 220 V 主电源用于洪水照明,还有工具等。各种形状连接叉连接举升点,或用改装的标准举升装置运输摩托车。

一些救援汽车装配成移动的修理间或是修理型货车,携带了许多工具、配件与修理设备,如千斤顶。近年许多还装有举升机折叠在汽车后门里面。

通讯

早期救援中,汽车驾驶员在汽车故障时用一些方法与俱乐部取得联系,有些机动车组织装有电话机,最终由代理为主要路网沿途安装电话,俱乐部巡逻队员也用俱乐部电话检查工作或在工作点等待呼救电话。五十年代,汽车无线电变得更加可靠,大多俱乐部和一些修理厂在汽车上安装无线电,这在紧急交通事故中作用很大,这样就有可能在救援车回来之前让其再次参与救援行动。

为实现这些装置的最佳使用,所有机动车组织在信息技术上投资巨大,根据就近设备、配件当然还有距离等因素,计算机软件依规范要求分配救援工作,这些车常装有 GPS 跟踪装置来传递当前位置信息。机动车组织的汽车也装有移动数据终端,让驾驶员直接知道具体细节。

大多汽车救援公司在 IT 上也要投资,多数有工作日志软件,很多装有车内通信装置和 GPS 跟踪装置,各环节工作分配是个十分技艺性的工作,参与人常有较大压力,在美国他们被称为调度员,在英国被称为控制器,因为期望救援者一天 24 小时接听电话,有时小救援公司几个小时后才能将电话接到信息服务中心。

Unit 13

Automobile Maintenance and Repair Tutorial

扫码获取
扩展视频

This tutorial is designed to assist the do-it-yourself with performing automobile repairs. It uniquely addresses maintenance and repair items at a summary level to provide a valuable supplement to detailed service and maintenance manuals. The goal is to support the do-it-yourself pursuing the goal of low cost, high quality, automobile transportation to the 200,000-mile vehicle life milestone and beyond.

Problem: Car Won't Start

If you turn your ignition key to the start position and your car won't start, the problem could be your starter. The starter turns the engine, so if your engine turns over, the starter is not bad. If the engine won't turn over, first eliminate other problems, such as:

Fig. 13 - 1 dead battery causes no starting

(a) A dead battery or corroded battery terminals. Turn on your headlights and interior lights, and then try to start your car. Have an assistant tell you if the headlights dim a lot, while you also watch the interior lights. If they do, and the engine won't turn over, suspect a bad battery or corroded battery terminals.

(b) A bad starter solenoid (if it is separate from your starter). If your battery and battery terminals are in good shape, you should hear the starter solenoid click once each time you turn the ignition to the start position. If not, suspect the solenoid. But before the final verdict, make sure there are not defective interlock switches, such as a park switch (with automatic transmissions) or a clutch switch (with manual transmissions) that prevent you from starting your car with gears engaged.

If your starter has over 50,000 miles on it, consider replacing it (as well as the starter solenoid), as preventive maintenance, or, quite possibly, to solve the problem. And if your battery is more than four years old, replace it too.

Problem: Engine Smokes

A worn engine can smoke because oil leaks into the cylinders around worn valve guides, or the oil rings are worn, or both. These conditions will create white smoke, which is burning oil, as opposed to a rich fuel problem, which will create black smoke, which is burning fuel.

If you get a puff of white smoke when you start your engine, after it has been sitting for hours, that's probably due to worn valve guides. Oil laying on the cylinder heads leaks into the cylinders while the car sits. Since the engine isn't running, the oil accumulates enough to cause visible smoke for a moment when the engine is started.

As long as the smoking engine doesn't foul spark plugs too often and can still pass emission tests, there's no big rush to do anything. You can plan this job, making arrangements for other transportation while the car is out of service. But don't procrastinate too long. If you do, you'll soon find yourself wanting to rid yourself of a clunker.

An engine that smokes (white smoke) is getting tired. It needs rebuilt... completely rebuilt. There's no sense in doing half a job. Bite the bullet and take your car or engine to your favoritc engine re-builder, or take it apart and go to your auto machine shop with the parts.

Don't attempt an engine rebuild yourself without good manuals and precision tools. And make sure you have the assistance of someone that knows what they're doing the first time.

Fig. 13 - 2 engine smoking

For some cars, exact factory replacement engines are available at a surprising good price. These are called factory crate engines. Not only are they brand new engines made by the car manufacturer, they carry a decent warranty. Check with your car dealer for this option. Then shop around between dealers, mail order and online suppliers to make sure you get a good price. You may find a large variation in prices.

Fig. 13 - 3 automatic transmission

Do not attempt to rebuild an engine in the car. You can't do the job right and you will probably risk injury. Get a quality engine lift and pull the engine.

Problem: Transmission Slips During Gear Shifts

An old automatic transmission often starts slipping between shifts. This can be due to worn clutch discs or bands.

If you're good at other car repairs, why not tackle an automatic transmission repair? A rebuild kit will set you back only a fraction the cost of a new or rebuilt transmission.

You'll probably need a day to pull the transmission (with help of an assistant), a day to take it apart, a day to inspect all the parts, a day to put it back together and a day to put it back in your car (with assistance again). If you've done this before, the time will be much less.

You'll also make a big mess with spilled transmission fluid so protect your garage floor with lots of newspaper and have lots of sawdust to soak up spills. You'll need lots of working surfaces to spread out all the parts in the order you remove them. A couple of cheap folding tables should do the trick if you need to improvise working surfaces. Finally, buy or borrow any special tools your manual calls for. If you're creative, you can probably improvise or even fabricate the special tools.

Above all, be patient and attentive to detail when rebuilding an automatic transmission, and follow a good manual step by step.

Problem: Air Conditioner Doesn't Cool

The simplest repair is replacing a broken or slipping compressor drive belt, so start with an inspection and/or adjustment of the belt. Next, check your refrigerant charge and add refrigerant if needed. You'll need an auto air conditioner pressure gage and a refill kit. You'll need to determine if your system uses the older R12 or the newer R134 refrigerant (look for a label under the hood). You must wear goggles when adding refrigerant to avoid being blinded if refrigerant gets in your eyes.

See if your air conditioner clutch engages and turns the compressor with the AC on and the engine running. If not, or if it cycles on briefly, then back off, the refrigerant charge may be low. Attach the pressure gage to the high-pressure line and monitor the pressure. If the AC clutch never engages, you may have to hotwire the clutch directly from the battery to make it engage. Once the clutch engages, see if the high pressure reaches the factory recommended value. If not, add refrigerant to the low pressure fitting, until the factory recommended pressure is achieved.

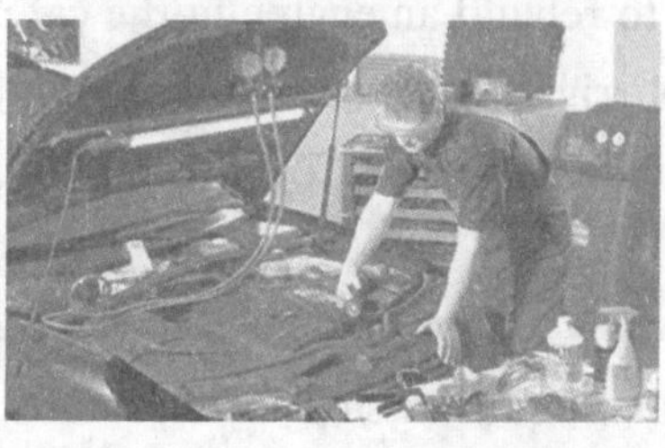

Fig. 13－4 air conditioner repairing

You can buy R134 in small cans at your local auto store, but you can't buy R12. If your system uses R12 and needs a charge, get out you checkbook and go over to the repair shop, since professional shops can still get R12 (it costs a small fortune). Before adding R12, the shop will probably insist on finding and repairing any leaks, adding to the costs.

If you have the older R12 system, you might want to consider converting to R134. A repair shop can do this (bring your banker along) or you can take a chance a do it yourself. Inexpensive retrofit kits are now available at your local auto parts store. The kits include high and low-pressure Schrader valve adapters (because R12 and R134 fittings are different), a can of a special R134-compatible oil charge, a refilling hose, and a couple cans of R134. Be sure you have a high-pressure gage that connects to the new R134 fittings. Remove the old R12. Be responsible and go over to the auto air conditioning shop to have the R12 removed, so as to not contribute to damage to the earth's ozone layer and get in trouble with the law. Follow the kit's instructions and install the R134 retrofit fittings on the existing R12 Schrader valves... then add the oil charge and the R134 charge up to the kit's recommended pressure. Don't expect a retrofit to freeze you out. R134 is not as good a refrigerant as R12, but it will do the job if the rest of the system is working OK. Also, professionals will probably advise you not to conduct this simple retrofit, insisting that you'll risk damaging your system with incompatible compressor oils. So you be the judge... pay their lofty price for a professional retrofit or do it yourself for next to nothing and risk a blotched job. If your AC doesn't work, and you can't afford to pay for a professional retrofit, and you can't take the heat, ask yourself if you have much to loose trying the retrofit. Ask around and you'll probably find people that got away with the do-it-yourself retrofit and are pleased with the results.

If you have a seized compressor or compressor clutch, and have some experience working with automotive air conditioning systems, go ahead and replace the compressor with a quality rebuilt unit (in some systems, it's best to replace the compressor and clutch as an assembly). Again, have the refrigerant professionally removed. Make every attempt possible to avoid having much air enter the system. Air does not compress easily and carries moisture. Both are a big problem. The moisture will condense inside the system and combine with refrigerant to create a corrosive acid that damages components. Air can overload the compressor and damage it. Any air and moisture that gets into the system must be drawn out with a vacuum pump before adding fresh refrigerant. So have a suitable vacuum pump ready or don't attempt the job. It is also advisable to replace the drier in your AC system. Its purpose is to capture any moister you missed with the vacuum pump.

NEW WORDS

tutorial	[tjuːˈtɔːriəl]	*n*.	使用说明书
manual	[ˈmænjuəl]	*n*.	手册
milestone	[ˈmaɪlstəʊn]	*n*.	里程碑
eliminate	[ɪˈlɪmɪneɪt]	*vt*.	排除
corrode	[kəˈrəʊd]	*vt*. & *vi*.	使腐蚀
solenoid	[ˈsəʊlənɔɪd]	*n*.	电磁开关
puff	[pʌf]	*vt*.	喷出
valve	[vælv]	*n*.	阀
procrastinate	[prəˈkræstɪneɪt]	*vi*.	拖延
clunker	[ˈklʌŋkə]	*n*.	破旧不堪的汽车
crate	[kreɪt]	*n*.	装货箱
clutch	[klʌtʃ]	*n*.	离合器
disc	[dɪsk]	*n*.	圆盘
bands	[bændz]	*n*.	带
tackle	[ˈtækl]	*vt*.	处理
sawdust	[ˈsɔːdʌst]	*n*.	木屑
soak	[səʊk]	*vt*.	吸入
spill	[spɪl]	*n*.	溢出量
gage	[geɪdʒ]	*n*.	压力计
refrigerant	[rɪˈfrɪdʒərənt]	*n*.	制冷剂
goggle	[ˈgɒgl]	*n*.	护目镜
leak	[liːk]	*vi*.	漏出
ozone	[ˈəʊzəʊn]	*n*.	[化]臭氧
retrofit	[ˈretrəʊfɪt]	*n*.	翻新
corrosive	[kəˈrəʊsɪv]	*adj*.	腐蚀性的
vacuum	[ˈvækjuːm]	*n*.	真空

PHRASES

dead battery　蓄电池亏电

REFERENCE TRANSLATION

汽车保养与维修指南

本指南用于帮助你自己修车,这里仅仅概要性地讨论下保养与维修的一些事项,作为详细的维修与保养手册的补充。目标是支持自修车者达到低成本、高质量,汽车里程达200 000英里以上的里程碑式使用寿命。

问题:汽车不能启动

如果你打开点火钥匙到启动位置而不能启动,问题可能在于启动器,启动器带动发动机,所以如果发动机能转动,起动机没有问题,如果发动机不能转动,首先排除其他问题,如

(a) 蓄电池亏电或接线端子锈蚀。打开前照灯和内部照明灯再启动汽车,让助手告诉你灯光是否变暗很多,同时自己观察车内照明灯是否变暗,如是的话,发动机不能连续转动,就需要检查是否蓄电池亏电或接线端子锈蚀。

(b) 启动机电磁开关故障(如是外置式的话)。如果蓄电池和接线端子没问题,你就要听一下每次点火开关打到启动档位置时电磁开关吸合时的咔嗒声。如果没有声音,检查电磁开关,但在最终确定之前,要搞清楚有没有互锁开关失效问题,比如停车开关(自动变速器)或离合器开关(手动变速器)失效会阻止你结合齿轮启动发动机。

如果你的启动机使用超过50 000英里,在预防性保养时考虑更换之(还有电磁开关),或者很有可能就解决了问题,如蓄电池使用超过了四年,也需要更换。

问题:发动机冒烟

发动机磨损会冒烟,因为机油从磨损的气门导管周围漏入气缸,也可能是活塞环磨损,或是两者都有。这种情况会冒白烟,而混合气过浓会冒黑烟,这是因为燃油没有烧尽。

在发动机停止几小时后,启动发动机时如冒白烟,可能因为气门导管磨损,在发动机停转后缸头漏出的机油进入气缸。因发动机并不转动,再次启动时机油积累得足够多引起一段时间能看到白烟。

只要发动机冒烟不会呛死火花塞而且能通过排放测试,没必要急着修理,你可以计划这事,在汽车过了保养期还可以安排运输任务,但不要拖延太久,否则的话,你不久就要将车抵成现金了。

如发动机冒白烟而无力,就要拆装了,彻底的拆装,局部修理是没用的,克服困难将车和发动机送到你相信的发动机修理厂吧,或拆开发动机带着磨损部件去汽车机加工厂吧。

没有详细的手册指导和精密工具,不要企图自己修理发动机,要确定你的助手真正知道怎么修理。

对有些汽车,可由制造厂换新发动机,价格还相当便宜,这叫原厂机,不但是全新厂

造发动机,还有可观的保障条款,与销售商联系这种换机方式,然后在各销售商间比价,写信订购或在线采购,确定你的价格合适,你会发现他们之间价差挺大。

不要企图在汽车上拆装发动机部件,这样做不好事情而且可能有受伤的风险,找一个质量好的举升机吊出发动机。

问题:变速器换挡时打滑

自动变速器使用久了后常会跳挡,这是因为离合器盘或带磨损。

如果你擅长修理其他类型车,为什么不开始自己修理变速器? 一套变速器工具的价格只是重修变速器或新变速器的一小部分。

你可能要花一天时间拉出变速箱(有助手帮忙),拆解一天,检查一天,装配一天,一天安装至车上(助手再次帮忙),但如果以前做过这事,花费的时间比这要少很多。

漏出的变速器油会将你的场地搞得一团糟,所以呢,要保护好修理工作面,用一些报纸和锯末屑吸油,你会需要很大的工作台来有条理地摆放拆解下来的零件,一些便宜的层叠式工作台有助于提高有效的工作台面积。最后,买些或借些手册上推荐用的专用工具。如果你够创新的话,还可以改进制作专用工具。

总之,按手册要求一步一步地,在拆装自动变速器时耐心地参与每一个具体过程。

问题:空调不制冷

最简单的修理是换有裂纹或打滑的皮带,所以先从检测调整皮带着手,接着检查充注制冷剂,如需要的话。你会需要空调压力表和充注接头,需要确定系统充的是老式的 R12 还是新式的 R134 制冷剂(查看发动机罩下的标签),必须要戴防护眼镜防止充注时制冷剂伤害眼睛。

看下空调离合器是否结合,空调压缩机是否工作和发动机工作情况,如没有问题,概略检查下空调循环,再回来查下,可能是制冷剂充注过少,压力表装到高压管线监控压力,如离合器没有结合,可以将离合器导线直接连到蓄电池使之结合,一旦离合器结合,看高压是否达到规定值,如没有,加注制冷剂到低压接头,直到达到厂标压力。

可以在当地汽车店里买小听装 R134,但不要买 R122,如你空调用 R12,去到修理店,再花钱买 R12,尽管专业的店里也仍可以买到 R12(它只需花费一小部分钱)。在充注 R12 前,商店里可能坚持要你找到和修理泄露点,这样会增加一些费用。

如果你的系统是老式 R12 空调,你会考虑换成 R134。修理厂可以做到(带一些钱)或者你有机会自己做。在当地零件商店你可以买到比较便宜的升级套装配件。套装包括高低压充注阀门适配器(因为 R12 和 R134 接头不一样),一罐与 R134 兼容的机油,一个充注管和几罐 R134。确保你的高压表连接到新的 R134 接头处。放完 R12。负责任些,去汽车空调店将 R12 换掉,以便不要损害臭氧层和违反法律。按照套装的说明在现有的 R12 充注阀上来安装 R134 改装接头……然后添加机油和 R134 达到套装规定的压力。不要期望改装的制冷效果太好。R134 制冷效果并不比 R12 好,但是如果操作得当,也足可以制冷。同样,专业人士会提议你不要进行这种改装,坚持认为会有不相宜的压缩机油损坏空调的风险。所以你要判断:是花高价专业改装 R134 还是自己改装但存在一定的风险。如果你的空调不能工作了,而你又负担不起高额的专业改装费用,你不能头脑发热,要问一下自己改装是否会失去太多。询问周围人自己改装的效果是否很满意。

如果你的压缩机和离合器有问题,而且你对汽车空调系统的维修也有经验,放心去用质量好的配件更换压缩机(在有一些空调中,压缩机和离合器是作为一个组件的)。并且,要有专业的方法泄放制冷剂。尽各种可能避免空气进入空调。空气不易压缩也有潮气。这两个都是很大的问题。湿气会在空调中冷凝,与制冷剂结合会产酸腐蚀损坏元件。空气会使压缩机过载而损坏。在添加新鲜制冷剂之前必须用真空泵吸出进入系统的空气和湿气。所以要准备好一个适合的真空泵否则不要企图进行修理。同样建议你更换空调干燥器,目的是消除真空泵没有抽出的那部分湿气。

Unit 14

When Is the Best Time to Buy a Car?

扫码获取
扩展视频

"The waiting game" is the least exciting way to pass the time, but if you're looking to get a good deal on a new car, then you're going to have to be patient.

Many people don't realize that carefully choosing when to buy your car can save you quite a bit of money. Well timed car purchases could save you thousands of dollars, if you play it just right. Here are a few tips to help you net that car you want-all while saving some precious money.

The Numbers Games

Dealerships and automakers award successful sales staff with money or perks for moving a certain number of vehicles during a given time period.

Fig. 14－1　waiting for a good time

Steve Emery, a consultant from the National Automobile Dealers Association explains that incentives can come from the automaker or within the dealership. Those issued by the automaker, are usually annually or quarterly, although monthly sales goals aren't uncommon either. Then each dealership has their own incentive program for their sales managers and sales staff. "They're like contests and can take place over a month," he says. "The incentives for the sales staff works in a stepped manner—if you sell 10 cars you get a \$500 dollar bonus all the way up to, let's say 15 cars gets you \$1,000."

Emery advises buyers to visit dealerships at the end of the month in order to gauge how hungry the dealership is to make a deal. If the salesperson is desperate to hit their target that month or quarter they may offer a few discounts, or forgo the usual lengthy process and headache when it comes to buying a new car.

Fig. 14－2　car sales soars

"The first place to start is the end of a particular month," he says. "Cars are sold on a 30 day cycle, so during the first few weeks, the sales staff are less inclined to work hard to sell you a car. They're taking a breath from the hot end of last month, and letting you browse. Then at the end of the month, when they're in a hurry to sell, they'll offer everything."

Emery also discusses that automaker incentive can change mid-month with no general announcement. "If a car isn't selling as strong at the beginning of the month, the automaker can say to the dealerships 'lower the lease price on this car.' The automaker doesn't have the time to advertise it, but the dealership will take care of it."

Waiting a Little Bit Longer

So while you should pay attention near the end of the month for incentives, some automakers offer huge quarterly incentives. Emery singles out Nissan as having huge quarterly sales goals which have an all-or-nothing attitude. "They ask dealerships to hit one lofty sales goal by the end of a quarter, offering them a huge bonus. But if they're one car under that, the dealerships get nothing," He says. "Those months which end on a quarter are big deals."

Waiting a Lot Longer

However, if you're looking for the best time in general to buy a new car, there's nothing like the end of the year. Annual sales targets provide a bigger bonus than monthly ones, so dealerships scramble to sell more cars during December in order to hit their numbers.

"Automakers have a plan and they commit to a certain number of models per year," explains Emery. "They can't tweak that very much, so it gets important to sell off all the models they can."

Fig. 14 - 3 car model update

Another reason that will make it easier to get a deal has to do with dealerships making room for new model-year vehicles. Even if a car isn't radically changed one year to the next, that older model year car be will tougher for the dealership to sell later down the road—they need to go now in order to make room for new cars. As a result, prices will drop, giving you more of an incentive to buy a car near the end of the year.

However, it's important to understand that at the end of the year you're picking at the leftovers. "Cars, colors and packages will be limited since all the good stuff sells first," warns Emery. "If you're looking for a mass market vehicle, and color isn't an issue, then the end of the year is a great time."

Year-end shopping will also be less competitive, forcing the sales staff to work on your terms. Consumers are usually tapped out near the end of the year with holiday gifts eating up most of the budget. This means showroom floors will be empty and sales people will be desperate to make a sale.

What If You Can't Wait?

If you can't wait until the end of the year, you may be able to get a deal just after summer or during the fall. Usually, this is when those new model year vehicles start to hit dealerships, meaning the time is ripe to make a deal. "When the new model comes out, you can easily get a deal on the last one, but you have to balance the discounts on the old model with the features of the new one," advises Emery.

Fig. 14 – 4 best time to get a good deal

The worst possible time to buy a car is in the spring. Buyers are excited after getting their tax refunds, and showrooms are busier during this time of the year. With so many people buying a car, it's harder to get a good deal during this time.

If you're looking to buy a car but want a good deal, be prepared to wait. First consider waiting until the end of the month, to see if the dealerships you're interested in are willing to make a deal.

Emery suggests looking for a car six months in advance, if possible. He suggests finding a dealership with an online sales department. "Send them an email saying you're not looking for a car right now, but would like to be notified of any incentives in the future," he says. He also suggests using sales groups like Costco or USAA, which are given all the details on current discounts and sales.

Armed with this information, it shouldn't be difficult to find a car at a price you can be happy with. Sure it might take some repressing of impulses, but the payoff will be worth it.

NEW WORDS

purchase	[ˈpəːtʃəs]	*n*.	购买
dealership	[ˈdiːləʃɪp]	*n*.	经销权
forgo	[fɔːˈgəʊ]	*vt*. & *vi*.	放弃
browse	[braʊz]	*vt*. & *vi*.	随意看看
incentive	[ɪnˈsentɪv]	*n*.	刺激
announcement	[əˈnaʊnsmənt]	*n*.	通告
scramble	[ˈskræmbl]	*vt*.	争夺

tweak	[twiːk]	*vt.*	用力拉
radically	[ˈrædɪkli]	*adv.*	完全地
refund	[ˈriːfʌnd]	*n.*	退款
showroom	[ˈʃəʊruːm]	*n.*	展厅

REFERENCE TRANSLATION

买车的最佳时间

“等待游戏”是消磨时间最没意思的一件事，但是要想新车买得便宜，只能耐心等待。

很多人并没意识到仔细选择购车时机会节约许多钱，时机正确会节约几千元，如何把握得准的话。以下的提示会有助你选择你想要的车，而且可节约你宝贵的金钱。

数字游戏

经销商和汽车厂商奖励成功的销售人员金钱或者补贴如果他们在规定时间内完成了一定的汽车销售量。

美国汽车销售协会顾问 Steve Emery 说这些刺激性的措施来自厂商或经销商，这些奖励通常是年度或季度的，虽然也有厂商会制定月度目标。每一个经销商对他们的销售经理和销售员都有自己的激励程序。“这些激励就像是竞争，每个月发生一次”，他说，“销售人员的激励以递进的方式进行。如果你卖 10 辆车，你可以得到 500 美元的奖励，卖 15 辆车可以得到 1 000 美元的奖励。”

Emery 建议买车人在月底去销售店看看销售人员表现出的想要完成一个订单的饥渴程度。如果销售人员急于完成月度或季度目标他们会给一些折扣，否则他就必须放弃这么长时间的销售目标和着急何时才会有人再来买车。

他说：“首先要做的是知道何时才是考核月的开始时间。卖车周期是 30 天，所以在头几个星期里，销售员卖车并不是非常卖力。他们要从上个月紧张的销售中喘一口气，并且让你随便看看。到月底，当他们匆忙销售之时，他们将给你能给的最低价格。”

Emery 也说汽车厂商刺激性措施可能会没有任何预告地在月中改变。“如果在月初卖车势头不是很强劲，汽车厂商会对销售人员说‘可以减少车辆的售价。’厂商没有时间预先通知你，但是销售人员必须预先考虑它。”

等待稍长时间

所以当你注意月底厂商刺激的时候，一些厂商却提供了更大的季度刺激。Emery 指出尼桑在有较大的月度销售目标时往往有不顾一切的态度。“他们让销售商在季末完成高不可攀的销售目标，给他们巨大的奖励。但是如果他们只差一辆车才能完成，销售人员将什么奖励也没有，”他说，“那些季度末的月份可买到最便宜的车。”

等得再久一点

然而，如果你期待在较长时间内的最佳时间能买到一辆便宜的新车，没有比年底更好的时期了。年度销售目标提供了比月度更多的奖金，所以销售员在12月份为达到目标数字尽力销售更多的汽车。

Emery说："厂商有年度计划完成一定数量汽车，他们不能差太多，所以很重视竭力销售达到目标。"

另一个原因是厂商希望销售商更容易完成销售，留出空间给来年新车型销售。尽管汽车不是每年都更新车型，但老车型对销售商来说更加难以销售，他们需要给新车型一定空间，结果，价格下降，年底会给你购车更多刺激措施。

但是，重要的是你要知道年底购车挑选余地较小，"车型、颜色和套件有限因为好的都已经先卖出了，"Emery警告说，"如果你希望买的是大众型车，颜色不是一个问题，年底是绝佳时机。"

年底买车竞争性不强，迫使销售人员按你的愿望销售。通常接近年底时，顾客已经没有多少余钱因为节日礼物差不多用光了他们的预算。这意味着展厅将会没多少人，销售人员需要外出销售。

如果等待不了该如何做?

如果你不能等到年底，你可以在夏季末或秋天买车。通常这时候新车型开始销售，意味着是买车的一个好时机。"当新车型推出时，你很容易以便宜的价格买到老车型，但是你必须在老车型的折扣与新车型的优势中寻求平衡，"Emery建议道。

春季是买车的最差时机。买车人在得到他们的返税后非常兴奋，展厅里是一年中最忙的时候。很多人买同一辆车，这时很难还价。

如果你又想买车又想便宜，只能等。首先考虑等到月底，看看你感兴趣的销售商是否会低价卖出。

Emery建议如果可能的话，提前六个月找好车型。他建议在网上找到销售商。"发邮件给他们说你并不需要立刻就买到一辆车，但如果将来有打折活动时就通知我，"他说。他也建议联系像Costco或USAA的销售集团，他们提供现有打折销售的全部细节。

借助于这些信息，不难找到令你满意的价格的汽车。当然你需要压抑自己的购买冲动，但是节约了钱也值得了。

Unit 15

What You Need to Know About Financing a Car

扫码获取
扩展视频

Buying a car is a tough financial commitment. It might take some help to get all the money for it, but that's exactly why car loans exist.

Getting a car loan is a relatively painless process, but there are quite a few steps involved that can make it a bit confusing to a first-time buyer. We've got you covered if you're looking for more information about getting a car loan, and what it all means to get saddled up with auto financing.

What Is a Car Loan?

Fig. 15 - 1 buy car by installment

If you don't have the \$20,000 or more to purchase a new car, you're going to have to borrow it from someone. When it comes to borrowing money for any circumstance, there's going to be a few terms about re-paying the loan. A car payment is separated into the principal amount and interest. Principal is the term used to refer to the actual amount of money being borrowed. While some financing deals offer 0 percent financing, other financing terms require you to pay interest owed on the loan amount.

Agreeing on a car loan also involves a length of time, normally in months of how you'll pay the borrowed money back. Car loan terms can be anything from 12 months to 72 months or even more in some cases. Knowing your budget and long-term financial situation should help you decide whether you can take a shorter term with higher payments, or a longer term with lower payments.

What Kind Of Car Lons Are There?

Fig. 15 - 2 how to choose cheaper loan

You can actually shop for a loan, and it's a good idea to look for a loan before you look for a car. Start by seeing your bank's interest rates and loan costs. Your bank will usually offer you a good rate since you're already a customer and they know your financial history.

A credit union is another place you can shop for a loan, which can be cheaper than the bank, but you may need to be a member. Homeowners may also take a home equity loan and pay for their car with cash, helping to reduce the pressure of interest on the car payments.

Finally, most auto manufacturers provide their own in-house financing companies at new car dealerships. These companies compete with the banks and credit unions. Remember though, the goal of these companies is to get you into their brand's cars, so they will likely offer the easiest and best car loan rates. When it comes to buying a used car, however, the dealership may have another financial institution to provide you with a loan, and often at a rate that benefits the dealer and not you.

Getting a good rate on your auto loan depends on your credit history. If you've missed payments in the past, or have a bankruptcy history, then you might not get a loan at competitive rates. Be sure to check your credit history before even shopping for a car loan, so you can correct any mistakes and get the best interest rate on your loan.

Long-Term vs Short-Term

It's important to understand how much you'll be spending on a longer term loan. While it does help reduce the monthly payments, you end up paying more money in interest. Some automakers offer online tools on their car-buying websites to see just how much more you'll be spending in interest over a longer term versus a shorter one. A shorter-term loan will result in your paying less in total over the course of the loan, than a longer-term one. That is, unless the financing offered is zero percent, in which case you'll pay the same amount whether the term is 36 months or 72.

Buyouts

If you have some extra money around, it never hurts to pay off the principal loan, but be warned not all financial institutions let you do so without any penalty. Since the company is potentially losing out on the remaining income from the interest, they may charge an early payout fee.

Fig. 15 - 3 read the loan items carefully

Insurance

Financial institutions will also require you to get some more comprehensive insurance for your car, though not as all-encompassing as a leased car. In some cases the financing company will need to be named on the insurance policy. Since the financial company has a financial interest in your vehicle until it's fully paid off, they will want it to be covered in case of any collisions or even a write-off situation where they would get paid. If a car gets written off in the first 24 months, its loan would be worth more than what the book value of the car is. This is a problem, and if you don't get "gap insurance" or a "waiver of depreciation", you may have to pay for that gap out of your pocket.

How Long Should You Finance a Car For?

More and more automakers are offering longer financing terms, but is it a good idea to commit to an eight year long auto loan, or is the dealer just out to get your money? It's always a good idea to get a budget sorted and have an idea of what your financial situation is before making a big purchase like a car. Fitting a car into your budget isn't always easy, which is why most new car buyers tend to mainly focus on a car's monthly payment. However, lower monthly payments can lead you into the trap of longer auto loans, and ultimately make you pay more for your vehicle.

This is due to interest rates. The longer your term, the more interest you pay on your loan. The numbers prove this point, and it's not a pretty picture.

The 2013 Nissan Altima SV has a MSRP (Manufacturer Suggested Retail Price) of \$24,870. Nissan offers 0% financing up to five years. Financing a car for three years after a \$3,000 down payment would give you monthly payments of \$608 a month. Compare that to a 75 month loan from Nissan which comes with a 4.59% finance rate. At just \$336 a month, monthly payments drop quite a bit. However, after the 75 month period the total amount of money that's been spent on the loan comes to \$27,450, and if you include the \$3,000 down payment you've paid \$5,580 more than the original MSRP of the car when it was brand new.

Fig. 15 - 4 how much should you pay a month

Despite the lower payments, you actually end up paying more for the total price of the car. To most savvy consumers, that's called a rip-off.

Longer loan periods also affect how you sell the car and what you can get back for it. For starters, you can only sell a car that is under your name, not when it's titled to the bank or a financial institution. Only after the loan is fully paid off can you sell the car.

Since cars are a depreciating asset, they're worth less money as they get older. At seven years old, you won't be able to sell a car for nearly as much as a five year old car. For example, a five year old car has lost about 55 percent of its original value, while a seven year old car loses 68 percent. That 2013 Nissan would return roughly $3,233.10 more if you sold it after five years, instead of after seven. Again, opting for a shorter loan period pays off where it counts, in your wallet.

Also, keep in mind the value of a car for a trade in. Some dealers will give excellent trade-in value to a car that can be certified and sold as a CPO car. However, very few automakers offer CPO cars that are seven years old, meaning there's a low chance of getting a good deal on a trade in.

NEW WORDS

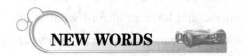

financial	[faɪˈnænʃl]	*adj*.	金融的
commitment	[kəˈmɪtmənt]	*n*.	承诺
credit	[ˈkredɪt]	*n*.	信用
union	[ˈjuːniən]	*n*.	联盟
bankruptcy	[ˈbæŋkrʌptsi]	*n*.	破产
versus	[ˈvɜːsəs]	*prep*.	与……相对
penalty	[ˈpenəlti]	*n*.	惩罚，罚金
collision	[kəˈlɪʒn]	*n*.	碰撞
savvy	[ˈsævi]	*adj*.	有见识的
depreciate	[dɪˈpriːʃieɪt]	*vt*.	使贬值
loan	[loʊn]	*n*.	贷款

REFERENCE TRANSLATION

贷款买车须知

买车要花一大笔钱。需要得到别人的帮助才能凑满这笔钱，这就是汽车贷款存在的理由。

得到汽车贷款过程不是很难，但对第一次申请贷款的人来说，也有几个步骤稍显迷惑。我们已帮你收集很多信息，提供你获得汽车贷款的几种途径。

什么是汽车贷款?

如果你没有20 000元或者更多去买新车，你就需要从别人那借钱。因种种原因需要借钱的时候，就有付贷款各种条款。汽车贷款支付分为本金与利息，本金指的是实际借钱的数量。有些信贷公司提供0利息贷款，而其他信贷公司需要你根据贷款额偿还利息。

贷款涉及贷款时间，还款一般以月度计算。汽车贷款时间从12个月到72个月，在有些情况下甚至更长。知道自己的预算和长期财务事项有助于你决定是选择短期贷款月度还款多还是长期贷款月度还款少。

有哪些汽车贷款类型？

实际上你可以贷款买车，建议在买车之前确定好哪种贷款。从银行利息与贷款费用开始考虑，如果你是它的老客户，借贷款历史信用较好，会给你优惠利息。

信用社是贷款的另一个地方，它比银行要便宜，但是你必须是会员。户主必须带上家庭贷款记录和买车的现金，有助于减少汽车贷款利息的压力。

最后一个是大多汽车生产商卖新车时会提供他们自己的贷款公司。这些公司与银行和信用社相互竞争。记住，公司的目标是让你买他们品牌的车，所以他们可能提供最低的和最好的贷款利率。但是当你买一辆二手车时，销售商在你贷款的时候给你的利息会高一些，并且利率有利于经销商而不是你。

贷款利率高低取决于你的信用历史。如果你有不及时还款或有破产记录，你的利息率会较高。在贷款前检查下信用记录，才可以纠正问题，在贷款时得到最优利率。

长期还是短期

知道长期贷款需付多少利息是很重要的。每个月还款额会减少，最终付息会比较多。有些厂商在他们的汽车购买网站上提供在线工具让你计算长期贷款比短期贷款最终多付多少利息。短期贷款与长期贷款相比可使总支付减少，除非是零利率，这时三年期和六年期支付总额相同。

提前还款

如果你有多余的钱，不妨碍你提前偿还贷款，但并不是所有贷款公司都不予以罚款地让你这样做，因为公司在剩余利息上有潜在损失，他们会收取提前还款产生的费用。

保险

贷款公司也会需要你购买一些比较综合性的汽车保险，虽然没有租车险那样什么险种都包括。有时，贷款公司要在保险条款上署名，因为在贷款支付完成之前，汽车上都有借贷公司利息部分，所以他们想在汽车发生碰撞事故时得到保险赔付充抵利息。如果汽车贷款要在头24个月内提前还完，贷款余额会比汽车账面价值高，这是个问题，如果你没有补偿差额险或折旧减免，你就需要自己出钱偿还差额。

应该选择多长时间的贷款

越来越多的生产商提供长期贷款，但采用八年期贷款是正确的吗？毕竟商人还是要赚钱的。在买像汽车这种大件之前，最好根据自己的经济情况做好分类预算。将汽车纳入预算不是件容易的事，这就是为什么大多数人买新车趋向于主要关注月度付款额。但是，较低的月还款使你陷入长期贷款，最终使你付款总额加大。

这是因为利率差的关系，期限越长，利息越高，最终的数字证明了这点，这个画面似乎不太美好。

2013 Nissan Altima SV厂商建议零售价MSRP是24 870元，尼桑提供最长至五年期无息贷款，三年期贷款首付 $3 000，月供 $608，而 Nissan 75个月贷款利率是

4.59%。月付336元，降了很多，但75个月后，还款额已达27 450元，如加上3 000元首付，你比原来的新车MSRP多付出5 580元。

尽管首付是低了，但实际上最终支付总额较高，对大多精明的消费者来说，这就是一种敲竹杠。

长期贷款也影响你卖车和最终车价，因为你只能卖你自己名下的车，而不是署名为银行或贷款公司的车，只有当贷款全清你才能卖车。

因为汽车是贬值资产，年限越久价值越少，使用七年的比五年的车卖的价要低，五年的车只有原值的55%，七年的车就要贬值68%。2013 Nissan五年后卖出价格约＄3 233.10，但七年后就没这么多了。还有，选择短期贷款付清后，钱就是你的了。

记住还有汽车以旧换新价值，有些经销商给的以旧换新价较高，可以CPO车售出，但几乎没有厂商提供七年期老车作CPO，意味着很少有机会在以旧换新时得到好的价格。

Unit 16

How to Park a Car

扫码获取
扩展视频

Parking Tips for Safety

It is important to know reference points to be looking for through your window to know how to park a car to keep from hitting obstacles and to get into the middle of your space.

This section will go over reference points for parking a car in all directions, even reversing into a stall. Parking lots have a lot of collisions because there are so many drivers and people, in such a small space. Backing up carelessly is the greatest cause of collisions in parking lots.

Move slow, but turn fast into your parking space. Moving slow allows you greater control in a small space and turning fast positions your car where you need it at the right time.

Fig. 16 - 1 so hard to park a car for green hands

Fig. 16 - 2 parallel parking

The speed you need to come into a stall is so low, just above 0mph, that once you start turning into the spot your foot should be covering the brake with just enough pressure to keep moving at this slow speed until you are straight in the stall.

There should be no need to use your gas pedal once you turn into the space unless you are coming uphill.

Look all directions continuously the direction you are moving when backing. This includes to the left, the right and directly behind your vehicle. As you are turning out of your stall, it's easy to remember looking to the sides but not behind.

this is where a car could be backing out opposite from you, or a pedestrian could be there.

Also don't take it for granted that no one will be behind you in a fairly empty, unused parking lot.

Many times, when practicing how to park a car with students in empty lots, we've seen not only cars speeding through, but also pedestrians and bicyclists.

Fig. 16 - 3 the hardest park—perpendicular

One other good rule to follow is to find a stall away from other parked cars, not so secluded that it makes you unsafe, but with enough space that you wont be in danger of hitting other parked cars or them hitting you.

Perpendicular Parking

Above is a picture of perpendicular parked cars. Cars parked straight in, on either side of a parking lot isle. This is probably the hardest parking to master after parallel parking.

Before turning into a stall, your easiest point of reference will be using your side mirror in relation to the FIRST line you approach of the stall you intend to enter.

Also be about 8 feet away opposite of the space you are aiming for, this makes it much easier to bring your wheels straight without bumping the curb.

Angle Parking

Parking a car in an angled stall is the easiest way to park a car. This is one reason many businesses choose to have angle parking in their lots. It also allows for more spaces than perpendicular parking stalls.

Parallel Parking

Parallel parking is the skill of parking between two cars parked beside the curb by aligning your car parallel with the car in front and backing between the two cars at a 45 degree angle into the parking spot.

It sounds hard and is probably the hardest parking to learn, however if you know what reference points to use, it's not as difficult as it seems.

Curb Parking

Curb parking is pulling to a curb in front of your vehicle or to the side of your vehicle. Using reference points will keep you from scraping the curb when parking at the curb.

How to Parallel Park:

Fig. 16 - 4 back slowly

Step 1.

As you drive past the parallel parking spot you intend to back into, size the spot with your vehicle to make sure it will fit. You want a space about six feet longer than your car. Be about four feet away from the car in front of the space you are backing into.

Step 2.

Line your steering wheel up with the steering wheel of the car before the space.

Step 3.

Next, look in the back passenger window on the side you will be parking.

You should see the rear of the car you are next to in the back part of the rear passenger window.

The top picture shows where you see the rear of the Echo in the back of the van window.

The window frame blocks the view of the very back of the Echo, but you can still tell where the back of the Echo is.

In this position you will clear the car in front when turning, while leaving room with the car behind.

Fig. 16－5 parallel parking picture

Fig. 16－6 look through the mirror

As you can see in the bottom picture, it's easy to see the rear of the vanin the back window of the Echo.

Step 4.

At this point you are ready to turn the steering wheel all the way to the right, letting off the brake a little, controlling your speed with the brake(unless you are going slightly uphill).

Remember two of the top most important parking rules: move slow and turn fast.

You turn right until you have a 45 degree angle with the car next to you as seen in the pictures below.

Notice with the van above it's a little less of an angle than with the Echo, this is because of the difference in the size of the vehicle.

Step 5.

Once you are at this 45 degree angle, turn your steering wheel fast about 1 revolution left(just enough to keep you at that angle). If you turn all the way left before backing up, you will end up too far from the curb.

Notice in this picture(using a Toyota Corolla and another parked vehicle), the front passenger seat is parallel with the corner of rear of the front vehicle. This is a fairly good reference point to know you have that 45 degree angle.

Step 6.

With your vehicle at a 45 degree angle(no more no less), start backing up slow until the side mirror is parallel with the rear of the car next to you as seen in the pictures below.

Some instructors say to use the steering wheel as a reference point instead of the mirror.

This works also, but I find using the side mirror is easier since it is outside near the parked car where you are already looking.

If your side mirror is at the rear of the car beside you, the front of your vehicle won't hit the parked car as you turn left.

Step 7.

Now look in your side mirror or out the window, to see how close you are to the curb. You may be a bit far away. If you are, back up until you see the mirror closer to the license plate of the parked car.

Step 8.

Once you are close enough to the curb, turn fast all the way left. This will bring the front of your car to the right, and using these reference points you should easily clear the car in front and have room with the car behind to straighten. If you believe you are getting too close to the car behind, go forward to get straight.

NEW WORDS

obstacle	[ˈɒbstəkl]	*n.*	障碍(物)
reverse	[rɪˈvɜːs]	*vt.* & *vi.*	(使)反转
stall	[stɔːl]	*vt.* & *vi.*	(使)熄火
collision	[kəˈlɪʒn]	*n.*	碰撞
spot	[spɒt]	*n.*	地点
pedal	[ˈpedl]	*n.*	踏板
pedestrian	[pəˈdestriən]	*n.*	行人

perpendicular	[ˌpɜːpənˈdɪkjələ(r)]	*adj.*	垂直的
bump	[ˈbʌmp]	*v.*	冲撞
curb	[kɜːb]	*n.*	路边

REFERENCE TRANSLATION

如何停车入库

安全停车贴示

知道如何从车窗找到参考点防止撞上障碍物倒入车位中间位置是很重要的。

这篇文章讨论从所有方向停车的参考点，甚至是倒车入库的参考点。停车场碰撞很多，因为在这么小的空间里有如此多的人停车，倒车不小心是停车场碰撞的最大原因。

慢倒车快转向进入停车位，慢慢倒车使你在空间小的地方更好地控制汽车方向，在恰当的时间内快速改变汽车倒车位置。

需要的进库速度很慢，只比0速快一点，一旦你进入转向点，你的脚应该放在刹车上给以适当的压力保持低速运行直到汽车直行进入车库。

一旦你进入转向位置，不需要踩油门踏板除非是在上坡。

倒车时不断四处观察，包括向左看向右看向后看。当你出车库时，很容易理解看向侧面而并不是后面，这时，可能有车与你相对倒出，或可能有行人在那儿。

同样地，不要想当然地认为在空旷的不太使用的停车场你的车后面没有人。

经常，学生们在空地上练车时，我们发现不只是有汽车快速通过，也有行人和骑自行车的人不时经过。

另一个很好的要遵守的原则是远离其他停好的车，不这样的话可能不安全，但如果空间足够你不会有撞到其他车的危险，他们也不会撞到你。

垂直停车

上面的图片是垂直停车。汽车直接倒车进入两侧都是停好的车辆。这可能是仅次于平行停车最难的停车方式。

在停车转向之前，最容易找到的参考点是用侧面后视镜看你接近的试图进入的车位的第一条线。

在离你观察的位置大约8英尺的地方会比较容易，你的车轮处于直线位置不会碰到路沿。

斜角停车

斜角停车是最容易的停车方式。这就是很多营业性停车场采用斜角停车位的原因，与垂直停车场相比可用空间更大。

平行停车

平行停车是在前后两车之间的路边停车技能，将你的车开至与前车平行然后倒车至两车成45°角的停车点。

听上去可能很难学会这种停车，但是如果你知道哪里是参考点就没有看上去那么难。

路边停车

路边停车是将车正对路沿停车或沿着路沿停车。使用参考点会防止你停车时撞到路沿。

如何平行停车

第一步：

当你开车到达平行的停车位置准备倒车，估计汽车倒车距离是否适合。你需要的距离比车身要长约6英尺。车后部与倒车位前车后部保持4英尺的距离。

第二步：

使你的车方向盘在前车方向盘之前。

第三步：

接着，从乘客侧后视镜向后看。

你应看到你的车尾与边车后排乘客窗平齐。

上图显示从这里可看见后排车窗。

后窗柱会挡住你的视线，但你仍可以知道后窗的位置。

在这个位置转向你可清楚看见前车，同时给后车留有距离。

如下图所示，很容易从后窗看见车尾。

第四步：

这个位置你可以打方向盘到最右侧，松开一点刹车，用刹车踏板控制速度（除非稍带上坡）。

记住下面两点是最重要的停车原则：慢车移动与快速转向。

如下图所示，将车向右打到与边车呈45°角。

注意到上面的车比这个角度要小一点，这是汽车长度的不同。

第五步：

一旦你处于45°角位置，向左快打方向盘一圈（足够保持这个角度）。如果你在倒车前向左打到底，你会停地离路沿太远。

图上可以看到（以丰田卡罗拉和另一辆车瑞丽为例），前乘客座位与前车后脚平行，这是45°角很好的参考点。

第六步：

使车保持45°角（不多不少），开始倒车直到侧面后视镜与边车后部平行如下图所示。

有些教练说用方向盘作为参考点而不是后视镜。

这样也行，但是我发现用后视镜较容易，因为它离你准备观察的边车距离比较近。

如果你的车后视镜在边车的尾部，你的车前部不会在你左转向的时候碰到边车。

第七步：

现在看侧后视镜或者窗外，观察离路沿的距离。你可能离得有点远。如果是的话，倒车直到你看见后视镜靠近前面车的车牌。

第八步：

当你靠近路沿的时候，快速向左打方向盘，这样会使你的车前部转向右侧。用这些参考点会使你很容易与前后车保持一段距离。如果你觉得太靠近后车，向前直行一点。

Unit 17

Tips For Driving a Car

扫码获取
扩展视频

In Flooded Areas

Floods can occur anywhere; therefore it is always useful to know how to drive safely through the flooder areas. According to a report in USA, most flood fatalities happen because people try to drive through the deadly waters instead of avoiding them.

Below-mentioned tips will help you be more careful in a touch situation:

Fig. 17 - 1 through flooded street

1. Do not drive through the standing water—Roads covered by water are prone to collapse and therefore you should strictly avoid driving through standing water. Additionally, attempting to drive through water may also jam your engine with an irreparable damage. If you can, you should always take an alternative route.

2. Should you face a flooded street, do your best to estimate the depth of water by carefully observing the cars that are passing through.

3. Drive slowly and steadily through the standing water.

4. Once you have crossed the flooded street, check the brakes of your car by gently pressing the brake by your left foot while maintaining speed with your right foot. This will dry the brakes of the vehicle and they should resume function as normal.

5. Modern cars come with air intake that is located low down at the front of the engine bay. Only a small quantity of water that is sucked in could cause a serious damage. The turbo-charged and diesel engines are most vulnerable to such damage.

Fig. 17 - 2 driving slowly

6. Consider driving in the middle of the flooded street as it is there where the water will be its shallowest.

We recommend that you get your vehicle checked if your car has been still for a long time in the flooded streets. The service centers or technician can advise you appropriately on how to repair any damage caused. If you happen to be in an area where there is no access to a technician and your car is stalled, you could remove the spark plugs (or injectors) and turn the engine over to expel any water from the cylinders before trying to start the engine.

In Monsoon

Here are few days away monsoon is coming in India. Monsoon comes with joy, happiness, water and also will bring difficulties for car drivers. In rainy season it is very hard to take care of your vehicle and drive without any harm. But few monsoon car care tips make it possible to keep your car safe in monsoon.

This monsoon season is very important for agriculture but not good for your car. You have to take extra care of your vehicle in rainy time. Cars in India now become a fashion and trend too. Many of peoples are using expensive and latest cars. But they are much worried about their vehicles in rainy season, because there is high chance for damage in this weather. There arc a few basic car care tips which can easily safe your car in monsoon season—

1. Never drive rush in the rain, it is very dangerous for you. Always drive slowly and carefully.

2. Before taking a turn always indicate with light torches. Extra care is required in rainy time.

3. There are pits in every where on the roads, so always try to stay far away from them. It is easy to take side from these pits and drive without hurry.

4. At the time of rain it is best suggestion to follow and don't try to overtake any other vehicles. Allow a car in front of you to make pave so you can easily drive in water to follow that.

Before preparing for monsoon, first of all make it sure that your car in perfect condition and there is no holistic lack in your car. So you should have to service your car and sure about that there is no problem in this. Always double check your cars important connections such as wiring, battery and other factors.

On Snow and Ice

Make sure your tires are in good condition with plenty of tread. This should be done early in the fall before the weather forecast says snow and ice is on the way. Tire rack.com suggests you should have 6/32nds of tread for snow and 4/32nds for heavy rain. This is at least twice as much tread as the legal limit of 2/32nds of tread.

Be sure your cooling system and antifreeze are working well. This winter driving tip should be done in spring before the hot weather as well as in the fall before the cold weather. If the radiator overflow jug is low, fill it up and find out why it is low. Checking your antifreeze. If there is a leak or a clogged radiator have it fixed. Also know when you need your antifreeze flushed out and replaced. Is it the green stuff that should be flushed every two years, or the pink stuff that can last as long as 10 years? Your mechanic can test the radiator fluid for a breakdown of properties that protect your radiator and engine.

Fig. 17 – 3 car care before winter

Is your car battery in good condition? Extreme heat from the summer can significantly weaken a cars battery, causing excessive discharging and corrosion. Since a battery needs more power to start in very cold weather, you want a fully charged battery with clean cables and terminals. If your battery is more than three years old it may be time to have your car battery replaced.

Do your wiper blades need replacing? If you have noticed your windshield wipers streaking, becoming extra noisy or the rubber separating from the blade, you are in need of a new set of wiper blades.

Are your brakes in good shape? Remember that on snow and ice stopping distance is at least twice as far as on dry pavement. It's very important to have brake pads and rotors that are not near the point of needing replacement in winter weather.

Also consider having your brake fluid flushed if you haven't in two years or more. Moisture can accumulate in the brake line not only causing rust but the moisture will vaporize from the heat when you apply the brakes causing less braking pressure and more stopping distance, something that could mean the difference between a collision and a safe stop on snow or ice.

Keep your vehicle in 1st or 2nd gear on snow or ice. A lower gear not only keeps your car moving slower, it gives the tires more power and more traction which is vitally needed on slick roads.

Put your vehicle in a lower gear when turning. Because of the weight shift on a turn it is much easier to lose control (even in dry weather) in the middle of a turn. It is very easy to skid even in 2nd gear on icy roads when turning, 1st gear is safest.

Use the gas pedal and brake pedal as gently as possible at all times on snow and ice. Any pressure on either pedal causes the weight of the vehicle to shift(Brake pressure sends weight to the front, gas sends it to the rear). This can cause a dangerous loss of balance and control on ice.

Push the gear in neutral to stop at red lights and stop signs. This is contrary to the teaching of safe driving practices but icy conditions require different driving than in dry or wet but non-freezing conditions.

Snow and ice are the only time I would suggest using neutral to help brake, and once you are stopped, immediately put the gear in 1st or 2nd again. Neutral disengages the engine from the wheels so the engine isn't moving the car forward. This brings a car to a stop much quicker on ice.

If you start to skid push the gear in neutral. Although I was driving slow and careful in 2nd gear, as I made a left turn my tires lost traction and I started skidding slowly toward a stopped car to my left headed the opposite direction. As soon as I put my car in neutral my car immediately stopped just about three feet from the other vehicle. This winter driving tip saved me from a collision.

NEW WORDS

fatality	[fəˈtæləti]	*n.*	死亡(事故)
tip	[tɪp]	*n.*	小窍门
prone	[prəʊn]	*adj.*	易于……的
irreparable	[ɪˈrepərəbl]	*adj.*	不能修复的
diesel	[ˈdiːzl]	*n.*	柴油机
vulnerable	[ˈvʌlnərəbl]	*adj.*	易受伤的
shallow	[ˈʃæləʊ]	*adj.*	浅的
monsoon	[ˌmɒnˈsuːn]	*n.*	(印度洋的)季风
holistic	[hoʊˈlɪstɪk]	*adj.*	功能整体性的
antifreeze	[ˈæntifriːz]	*n.*	防冻液
jug	[dʒʌg]	*n.*	壶
wiper	[ˈwaɪpə(r)]	*n.*	雨刷
windshield	[ˈwɪndʃiːld]	*n.*	〈美〉汽车挡风玻璃
disengage	[ˌdɪsɪnˈgeɪdʒ]	*vt.*	分开

REFERENCE TRANSLATION

行车注意事项

在涉水区域

洪水哪里都可能有，所以最好知道怎么在涉水路面开车，按美国统计，大多涉水死亡事故是因为人们试图开车通过致命水域而不是避开它。

下面的提示将帮助你在遇到情况时更加小心：

1. 不要驾车通过积水——被水覆盖道路很容易倒塌，因此你应该严格避免驾车通过积水。此外，试图通过水流也可能堵塞你的发动机造成不可修复性损坏。如果可以，你应该总是采取替代路线。

2. 你可能要面对积水的街道，你最好仔细观察正在通过的汽车，估计水的深度。

3. 开车慢慢匀速地通过积水。

4. 一旦通过涉水街道，用右脚保持车速，左脚轻踩刹车来检查刹车，这样做会弄干刹车片以保持它们的正常功能。

5. 现代汽车的进气口位于发动机托架的前下部。只要吸入少量的水就可能造成严重的损伤。涡轮增压和柴油发动机最容易受到这种伤害。

6. 考虑在被洪水淹没的街道中间驾驶因为路中间积水最浅。

如果你的车在街道的洪水停放很长一段时间了，我们建议您检查汽车。服务中心或技术人员可以建议你适当如何修复受损件。如不巧汽车抛锚的地方，联系不到维修技师，你可以拆除火花塞(或喷油器)，多转发动机几圈将水排出去，才能启动发动机。

在季风天气

印度过几天就是季风季了，季风带来了兴奋、快乐、雨水，也给驾驶带来了困难。在多雨季节，汽车的驾驶和保养很难不受影响，但很少有季风时的汽车保养提示让你可能在季风季使汽车保持安全状态。

季风对农业很重要，但对汽车并不好，在雨季要特别照顾好车辆，汽车现在在印度也成为一种时尚和趋势，许多人使用的是昂贵的和最新型的车，但在多雨的季节他们很担心他们的车辆，因为这种天气很可能造成损伤，这里有一些季风季基本的汽车保养的小窍门。

1. 下雨不开快车，这对你很危险。总是小心慢慢地开。

2. 转弯前总是打转向灯，在下雨的时候需要额外的小心。

3. 道路上随处有坑，所以总是尽量远离它们。开慢车很容易绕过这些坑。

4. 在雨天最好建议你跟随前车，不要试图超越其他车辆。让你前面的汽车为你探路，这样跟着它你可以很容易地涉水通过。

在为季风季来临前做准备工作之前，首先保证汽车工况良好，总体性能没有缺陷，所以要做个保养确定没有问题。总是双重检查汽车重要连接如导线、蓄电池和其他部件。

在冰雪天

确定轮胎状态良好、纹理深度足够，这需要早在秋天天气预报说冰雪天快到之前就要做好。Tire rack.com 建议的胎纹深度是雪天 6/32nds，大雨天 4/32nds。这是至少法律限制的 2/32nds 的两倍。

要确保你的冷却系统和防冻正常，冬季驾驶准备应该在炎热天气之前的春天和寒冷天气之前的秋天做好，如果散热器溢流水箱液位低，加满并找出它低的原因。检查防冻液。如果散热器有泄漏或堵塞，需维修，也要知道多长时间需要更换防冻液，防冻液是绿色的、每两年应换一次吗？或是粉红色的吗？红色可使用十年。你的机械师可以测试防冻液属性，以保护你的散热器和发动机。

你的车电池的状况好吗？夏天的酷热会大大削弱汽车电池，造成过度放电和腐蚀。由于电池在很冷的天气需要更多的能量用于启动，你需要充满电的电池和干净的电缆和接线端子。如果你的电池超过三年时间可更换电池。

你的雨刮器需要更换吗？如果你注意到雨刷快速移动并发出额外的噪声或者刮片橡胶分离，你需要一个新的雨刮片。

你的刹车状况好吗？记住，在雪和冰上的停止距离至少是在干燥路面的两倍，在冬季刹车片和刹车盘不处于需要更换的临界点附近是非常重要的。

同样如果你两年或以上没有更换刹车油，考虑更换。水分会在刹车管线中积累导致生锈，踩刹车时产生的热量使水挥发而减少刹车压力，停车距离变长。水分也会使在碰撞和安全停车时刹车表现有所不同。

在雪地或冰面上，保持你的车在第一或第二挡。低挡不仅保持您的车缓慢移动，也给轮胎更多的动力和牵引力，这在光滑的道路上是非常必要的。

让你的车低挡运行。在转弯中间，因重心偏移，易于失去控制（即使在干燥路面），冰面上二挡转弯容易打滑，一挡最安全。冰雪路面任何时间尽可能轻踩油门踏板和制动踏板；任何踏板上压力稍大会使车辆的重量转移（刹车使重量偏向前，油门使重量偏向后），这样会在冰面上引起失去平衡的危险。

在到红灯和停止线前就将车挂在空挡。这是违背安全驾驶教学的行为，但在冰面上与干或湿的但非冻结的路面上需要不同的驾驶方法。

在冰雪路面，我才会建议空挡踩刹车，再快速切换到一或二挡。空挡发动机与车轮不连接，所以发动机不会驱动汽车前行，这使车在冰冻路面上快速停车。

如你开始打滑，将挡位打到空挡，虽然我以二挡慢慢开车，可当我左转时轮胎失去牵引力，我的汽车左前部慢慢地滑向一辆相对方向停止不动的车，我马上挂空挡，汽车立即停了下来，刚好离那辆车只有三英尺远，这个冬季驾驶技巧使我避免了一次碰撞。

Unit 18

Driving in America

扫码获取
扩展视频

Always be careful to never miss your exit. If you miss your exit, do not stop and never back up on the highway. Get off the highway at the next exit and look for signs showing you how to rejoin the road in the other direction.

Fig. 18 - 1 traffic signs

Freeways have emergency call boxes at regular distances from where you can report an emergency or a breakdown. All freeways have right-most lane demarcated as the break-down lane. Stop your car in that lane. Never drive in that lane.

In case your car breaks down on a freeway, if you have a mobile phone call 911. You can also open the bonnet of the car and wait for someone with cell phone to report your emergency. This is common and if you have a cell phone and see such a site, you too should call 911 and report it. You can also carry a large sign that says, "Call Police—Send help" in case of a breakdown.

Alcohol can only be transported in the boot of the car, because it is illegal to carry it in the car cabin. It goes without saying that you can not drink alcohol while driving. Traffic laws are set by states and regions, but in general the interstate speed limit around the country ranges from 55 to 65 miles per hour. The speed limit in cities is usually set between 25 and 30 miles per hour. Speeding is a serious offence resulting in high fines.

You should always carry with you your local license along with IDP when driving in a foreign country.

If you live in region where it snows, do keep the snow shovels to be kept in cars, along with a torch (preferably with a blinker built in), a blanket, spare gloves, etc. These come handy if the car breaks down during cold nights on highways or if one needs to change the flat tire.

Fig. 18 - 2 stop before cross way

You should, at least once, change the tire of your car during day time as a practice drill. This will help you in gaining some confidence and you don't find it difficult when you actually are stuck in such a situation.

If you have met with an accident, don't panic. Relax. The worst is over. Take the license, insurance details of persons involved, and witnesses. Call the police and don't leave that spot till a cop arrives. Keep your insurance details (your insurance number and phone of the company you are insured with) in the car.

AAA (called triple-A) is a very active organization for the road safety and trip planning. They provide lots of other facilities too. Being a member of AAA is a good option especially for new comers.

Typical Traffic Rules

Keep Right

The traffic follows the "keep right rule". While driving, drive on the right side of the road. On one way, multiple lanes road, the right-most lane would be slowest and left-most lane is fastest.

Hand Signals

Though indicators are used for the purpose of showing which direction we are going, knowing the relevant hand signals is very important and are usually always asked in a driving test. When we want to turn right, we can put our left hand out of the window and point upward. When we want to make a left turn, we can stick our left arm out of the window and point to the left. If we want to slow down or stop, we can just point downward.

Fig. 18 - 3 yellow school bus

The Turning Lanes

On some two-way roads, a center lane may be marked as a common left-turn lane to be used by vehicles in both directions. You may only use this type of lane for turning left. You may not travel in a center turning lane.

School Buses

Yellow school buses have flashing red lights and stop signs that fold out from the driver's side. School pupil transport vehicles, like vans, station wagons, or family sedans, have flashing red lights and SCHOOL BUS signs on top. Drivers of either kind of school vehicle use these warning signals when letting pupils on and off. No matter which side of the road you are traveling on, if you come upon a school bus or a school pupil transport vehicle with its lights flashing and a stop sign extended, you must stop. It's the law. Remain stopped until the lights stop flashing or the stop sign folds back.

Using the Horn

Using horns is not common in America. Actually they are very rarely used. You may use your horn to warn pedestrians or other drivers of possible trouble or to avoid accidents. Do not use your horn to express anger or complain about other drivers' mistakes or to try to get a slow driver to move faster.

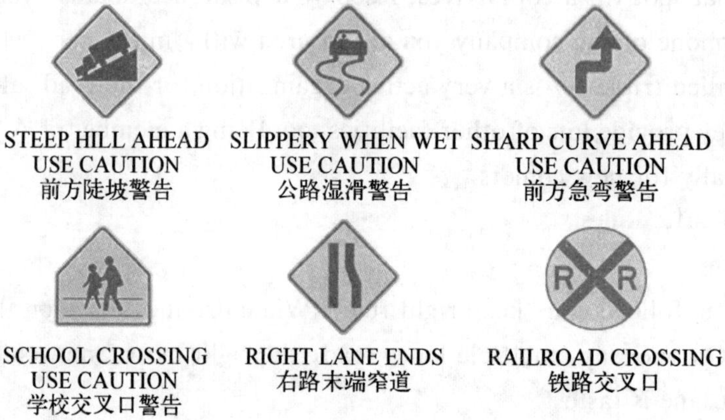

Fig. 18 - 4 kinds of signs

Yielding

When you see a YIELD sign, slow down and be prepared to stop. Let traffic, pedestrians, or bicycles pass before you enter the intersection or join another roadway. You must come to a complete stop if traffic conditions require it. When taking left turn on a green light in a four way intersection, you must first yield the right-of-way to any oncoming vehicle. You can roll ahead to the middle of the intersection, wait till there is no oncoming traffic and turn left. If there is a continuous stream of oncoming traffic, wait till it is a red light for the oncoming traffic. There is a delay till the green goes up for the other side and you can make your left in the meantime.

Stop

An eight-sided (octagon) sign tells you to always make a full stop. You must make a complete stop at the stop line. If there is no stop line, stop before entering the crosswalk. If there is no crosswalk, stop before entering the intersection. Yield the right-of-way to pedestrians and closely approaching traffic. If it is a 4-WAY STOP sign, wait your turn. 4-WAY STOP sign means there are four STOP signs at the intersection. Traffic from all directions must stop. The first driver to stop is the first driver to go.

High-Occupancy Lanes

A white diamond alerts you to a special lane restriction, like "high-occupancy vehicle" (HOV) only. These lanes are only for vehicles having more than one occupant. Since, more than one occupant in a car is very rare in America, especially in peak hours, this lane has very less traffic. This is to encourage car pooling.

Traffic Policing

If stopped by a police officer for a traffic violation, do not argue. Apologize for doing anything wrong. Mistakes happen. He may let you off for a genuine mistake, but not for a serious violation. You might still receive a traffic ticket if you're nice. To antagonize the officer is not a best thing to face. Do not attempt to bribe an officer, or you could be arrested for a crime.

NEW WORDS

demarcate	[ˈdiːmɑːkeɪt]	*vt*.	定……的界线
bonnet	[ˈbɒnɪt]	*n*.	发动机盖
shovel	[ˈʃʌvl]	*n*.	铲子
glove	[glʌv]	*n*.	手套
indicator	[ˈɪndɪkeɪtə(r)]	*n*.	指示灯
wagon	[ˈwægən]	*n*.	货车
sedan	[sɪˈdæn]	*n*.	〈美语〉小轿车
horn	[hɔːn]	*n*.	喇叭
pedestrian	[pəˈdestriən]	*n*.	行人
crosswalk	[ˈkrɒswɔːk]	*n*.	人行横道
lane	[leɪn]	*n*.	车道
occupant	[ˈɒkjəpənt]	*n*.	占有者
genuine	[ˈdʒenjuɪn]	*adj*.	真诚的
antagonize	[ænˈtægənaɪz]	*vt*.	引起……敌对

REFERENCE TRANSLATION

车行美国

时刻注意不要在高速公路上错过了出口！但是如果你错过了，也不要停下来，更不要倒回去，只需在下个出口处离开，并寻找那些能告诉你如何从另一个方向再上高速公路的指示牌。

高速公路每隔一段距离都有紧急电话，你可以打电话报告紧急情况或汽车故障。所有高速公路都将最右边的车道划为故障车道。你可将故障车停在这个车道。这个车道从不用于行车。

你的车抛锚时，如果你有移动电话可打911。你也可以打开车盖，等待有手机的人来为你打电话报告紧急情况。这很正常，如果你有手机看到这样一种情况，你也应打911报告。抛锚时，你也可以举一个大牌子写道，"打电话叫警察来帮忙"。

酒精类饮料只能装在行李厢里，因为放在驾驶室内是违法的。毫无疑问，你不能一边开车一边喝酒。交通法规是由国家和地区制订，但在美国一般的州际公路速度限制的范围从55到65英里每小时。城市里的车速限制是通常设置25和30英里每小时之间。超速行驶会造成高罚款严重违法。

在国外开车时你应该总是随身携带你的本地 IDP 和驾照。

如果你住的地方经常下雪，务必在行驶时带上雪铲、手电(最好装有警戒灯)、毛毯、备用手套等东西以应急。寒冷的夜里，当车在公路上抛锚或需要换车胎时，这些东西用得着。

你应该至少有一次在白天练习更换您的汽车轮胎，这将帮助你获得一些信心，当你真正遇到此种情况你不觉得有什么困难，

如果你遇到车祸，不要惊慌，保持镇定，最糟的时刻已经过去了。准备好你的驾照、个人保险材料，并找到目击者，然后打电话报警。在警察到来以前，不要离开现场。在车里随时带着你的保险材料，包括投保号、投保公司的电话号码等。

AAA(称为3A)是道路交通安全和旅游规划的一个非常活跃的组织。他们也提供很多其他服务设施。成为 AAA 成员尤其对新来的人是一个不错的选择。

典型的交通规则

右行

交通遵循"靠右"原则。开车的时候，在路的右边开车。行驶在一条车道上，多车道的道路，最右边的车道往往是最慢的，最左边的车道是最快的。

手语

虽然指示灯可用来显示汽车行驶的方向，但了解一些常用的手势语也很重要，而且在驾驶考试中经常被问到。当你想向右转弯时，将左手伸出窗外并指向上方；向左转时，伸出左臂指向左边；如果想减速或停车，只需向下指就行了。

转弯车道

在一些双向公路上，有一个中心区域被划为左转车道，以供来往车辆使用。但这条道只能用于左转，不能在中心转向车道上行驶。

校车

黄色校车有闪烁的红灯和停车标志牌折叠安装在驾驶员侧。学校接送学生的车辆，如厢式车，旅行车，家庭轿车的车顶都有闪烁的红灯和校车标志。学生上下车时，无论哪种校车的驾驶员都使用这些警告标志。无论你行驶在路的哪边，如果遇见那些闪烁着红灯或伸出“停止”字样的校巴，你都得停下。这是法律规定的。你必须等灯熄了或标志牌收回后，才能开车。

使用喇叭

使用喇叭在美国是不常见的。事实上它们很少被使用。你可以用你的喇叭警告行人或其他可能有麻烦的司机，或者为了避免车祸。千万不要用它来发泄怒气或对其他司机表达不满或催促你前边的司机加速。

让路

当你看到一个让路标志，减速并准备停车。在你进入十字路口或驶入另一条马路之前，让交通、行人或自行车通过，如果交通条件需要的话，你必须一直等下去。在十字交叉路口，绿灯亮左拐的时候，你必须先让出右行道给任何迎面而来的车辆。你可以开到十字路口中间，等到没有迎面而来的车辆时再左转弯。如果迎面而来的车流连续不断，等到对面交通亮红灯。红灯与另一方向绿灯亮之间有一个延迟时间，其时你可以左转。

停止

八边形标志意味着你必须在停车线处完全停止；如果没有停车线，就在你驶入人行道之前停车；如果没有人行道，就在驶入十字路口前停车，把道路右边让给行人和迎面驶来的车辆。如果是一个四向停车标志，你就得停下来。四向停车标志表示在十字路口上有四个停车标志。各个方位的车都必须停止，先停的车辆先走。

多乘客车道

车道上的白色菱形标志提醒你这是一个特殊车道，如“HOV满员车专用”，这种车道专供有一个以上乘客的车辆行驶，因为在美国车上多于一人的情况很少，特别是在交通高峰时刻，这条车道的车非常少。这也是鼓励拼车的一种方法。

交通警察

如因违章被一个警察拦住了，不要争论，为做错事道歉，错误发生了，真诚承认错误他会让你走的，如不是很严重违规的话。如果情况不错的话你可能收到交通罚单，对抗警官不是面对事情最好的办法。不要试图贿赂官员，否则你可能因犯罪而被逮捕。

Unit 19

2019 Honda Civic vs 2020 Toyota Corolla
—Who Will Be Crowned King of the Compacts?

扫码获取
扩展视频

When it comes to compact cars, two models have dominated the segment over the past several years. The Honda Civic and the Toyota Corolla are in a constant battle for sales supremacy. Last year Honda unveiled an all-new Civic that handily outsold the ancient 2019 Toyota Corolla despite a lukewarm reception.

But this year, Toyota has a new Corolla, one that is a drastic departure style-wise from every Corolla before it. Not wanting to sit back and watch this new "corolla" outpace the Civic on the sales chart, Honda expedited a refreshed Civic only one year after introducing an all-new new model. The manufacturer has taken to heart the criticism both from consumers and the automotive press lambasted on the 2018 Civic.

Reresh vs Revolution

One of the biggest issues with the 2018 Civic redesign was how closely it resembled the previous generation. After such an extreme redesign in 2012 people expected more with the new Civic; a lot more. So, for 2018 Honda added some plastic chrome here and there, a new set of taillights, a few more muscular creases. A more modern, if not attractive, Civic was born.

Toyota may have been watching the backlash the 2018 Civic received and decided to throw all of its proverbial cards on the table when sculpting the 2020 Corolla. This car is a grand departure from past models and features bold, aggressive styling. Yes. A bold Corolla. We'll let that sink in for a moment.

The new car is more round, modern and eye catching. Our Corolla S test model came with the optional two-tone 17-inch wheels that remind us of those found on the Scion FR-S. Like many compact cars these days, the new Corolla has a large gapping grille flanked by angry looking headlights. Unlike any compact car on the market today, or hardly any car at price, the Corolla comes standard with LED headlights.

Technology vs Luxury

As dramatic as the exterior restyle may have been, the interior is what really grabbed our attention. Toyota really had nowhere to go but up with the Corolla's interior, yet still delivered beyond our expectations. The modern design integrates all the switch controls in a seamless and appealing way. The multi-angle dashboard looks more upscale than expected in a car at this price point and beside the Civic's drab interior, it looks downright stylish.

Fig. 19－1 Toyota Corolla

But Honda did make several changes to the 2019 Civic's interior as well. Most materials were upgraded including a deeper grain plastic on top of the dash and the soft materials for the door tops as well as a strip on the glove box. The entire center console is all-new and now includes Honda's multi-screen display on higher trimmed models. This layout works especially well because it allows you to see music information and the navigation screen simultaneously. With the digital gauges and multiple color displays, the Civic's driver-focused dash is more tech-heavy than the Corolla's.

The Corolla blows away the Civic as well as several mid-size sedans, by offering 41.4 inches of rear legroom. Yup, that is over five inches more than the Civic and nearly as much as Toyota's own Camry. With 13.0 cubic feet of cargo room in the trunk, the Corolla also trumps the Civic by a half cubic foot of space. In such a pragmatic segment, this is how you win customers.

Power vs Transmission

By now you may have noticed we have yet to mention what powers either of these cars or how they drive. That is because neither the Civic nor the Corolla offers much new or all that exciting under the hood. Powering all non-Si Civics is still the same 1.8-liter four-cylinder engine making 140 hp and 128 lb-ft of torque. It can be matched up to a five-speed manual transmission in the base LX Civic while every other trim offers a five-speed automatic only; proof that the Civic's days as a sport compact are long behind it now (Si not withstanding).

The Corolla also uses a 1.8 liter. The new trim features Toyota's Valvematic technology to improve fuel efficiency and bump power up to 140 hp. Speaking of technology, the four-speed automatic is still technically available, but reserved mostly for fleet sales in the base L model. All other Corollas will come with a CVT while the base L and "sporty" S can be had with a six-speed manual.

Same on Paper, Different in Real Life

Fuel economy looks to be a dead heat for our comparison vehicles. The Civic EX-L is officially rated at 28 mpg city and 39 mpg highway, while the Corolla S is rated to return 29 mpg in the city and 37 on the highway. But that is on paper. In the real world a clear winner emerged; the Corolla averaged 34.6 mpg while the Civic could only 33.1 mpg.

Thanks to the low dashboard and belt line, the Civic offers great sightlines all around, but some of our taller drivers found the seating position a bit too high. Conversely, the high-set dashboard in the Corolla made it difficult for some of our shorter drivers to gain optimal forward visibility.

Fig. 19 - 2 fuel economy

The Corolla's responses feel even further dulled down as the steering and throttle are no particularly quick to respond. The engine is a bit noisy when paired with the CVT, but is quick to modulate rpm and in sport mode can be run through seven simulated gears.

The Verdict

The Civic begins at a price of $ 18,995 which is $ 1,385 more than the base Corolla. Our fully added Civic EX-L with Navigation rang in at $ 24,922 after destination charges while the Corolla S Premium costs $ 23,570. Our Civic also had a set of dealer installed 17 inch wheels not listed here that would ramp the price up even further.

Although the Civic may have a slight edge in the driving department, it's the more practical features of compact sedans that consumers really care about. Factors like price, fuel economy and space top their priority lists and the Corolla trumps the Civic in those categories. In such a close race, that's more than enough to hand it the win.

NEW WORDS

segment	[ˈsegmənt]	*n*.	部分
unveil	[ˌʌnˈveɪl]	*vt*.	揭开
drastic	[ˈdræstɪk]	*adj*.	猛烈的
chart	[tʃɑːt]	*n*.	图表
lambaste	[læmˈbeɪst]	*vt*.	严责
chrome	[krəʊm]	*n*.	铬合金
backlash	[ˈbæklæʃ]	*n*.	反击
sculpt	[skʌlpt]	*vt*.	雕刻

dashboard	[ˈdæʃbɔːd]	*n*.	仪表板
drab	[dræb]	*adj*.	单调的
stylish	[ˈstaɪlɪʃ]	*adj*.	流行的
console	[kənˈsəʊl]	*n*.	控制台
legroom	[ˈlegruːm]	*n*.	供伸腿的空间
pragmatic	[prægˈmætɪk]	*adj*.	实用主义的
sightline	[ˈsaɪtlaɪn]	*n*.	视线
throttle	[ˈθrɒtl]	*n*.	节流阀
trump	[trʌmp]	*n*.	喇叭

REFERENCE TRANSLATION

2019本田思域 vs 2020丰田花冠
——谁是紧凑型车王?

说到紧凑型车，在过去几年两分市场占主导地位。本田思域和丰田花冠都在为销售的优势不断战斗。去年推出的全新本田思域销售大大超过先前的2019丰田花冠，尽管反应冷淡。

但今年，丰田有一个新的花冠，与以前的花冠相比风格发生了急剧变化。不想坐等看到新"花冠"超过思域的销售图表，在推出全新车型仅一年后，本田快速升级新思域，制造商采取耐心听取来自消费者的批评和汽车媒体对2018思域的抨击。

升级与革命

重新设计2018思域最大的问题是与上一代的接近程度。在2012这样大的重新设计之后，人们对新思域期待很多、非常多。所以，2018本田多处添加塑料镀铬，一套新的尾灯，更有力道的线条！如果说不够吸引人的话也算是更加现代的思域问世了。

丰田可能已经看到2018思域的反击，决定重塑2020花冠在桌上打出所有的底牌。这辆车与过去车型截然不同，设计大胆、具有野性的风格。是的。一个大胆的花冠。我们会让对手瞬间沉没。

新车更圆，更现代和更醒目。我们花冠的S测试车型来了，可选的双色17英寸的车轮提醒我们这可是曾装在Scion FR－S车的。像现在许多紧凑型轿车一样，新花冠有较大间隙的格栅，侧翼大灯看起来很张扬。不同于今天市场上任何紧凑型车，或很少有这个价格的车在标配LED头灯，花冠这样配了。

技术与豪华

外观重塑可能已很戏剧性，内部才是真正吸引我们的注意力的所在。丰田真的除在花冠内饰做文章外没有别的办法可想。但最后效果仍然超出我们的期望。现代设计以无缝的和有吸引力的方式集成了所有的开关控制。多角度的仪表盘看起来比预期的这个价位汽车和旁边思域的简陋的内饰更高档，看起来很时尚。

但是本田同样对2019思域的内部做了一些改变。大多数材料得到升级，包括更深的纹理塑料仪表板和车门上的软质材料以及手套箱带。整个中控台是全新的，包括高配本田的多屏显示。这种布局效果特别好，因为它让你同时看到音乐信息和导航屏幕。配以数字仪表和多彩显示，思域的面向司机的仪表板比花冠更重视科技。

花冠打败思域以及一些中型轿车，提供41.4英寸的后排腿部空间。是的，这超过思域五英寸以上，几乎和自己的丰田凯美瑞一样。货物空间为13立方英尺，花冠还超过思域半立方英尺的空间。有这样一个实用的空间，是其赢得客户的原因。

发动机与变速器

现在你可能已经注意到我们还没有提到动力，无论是汽车还是驱动方式。这是因为无论是思域还是新花冠都没有提供多少新的或令人兴奋的发动机。提供所有非SI思域的仍然是相同的1.8升四缸发动机，提供140马力和128磅英尺的扭矩。基本型LX匹配五速手动变速器，其他配置只配五速自动变速器，证明现在思域还可以在今后长时间内作为紧凑型运动车(Si除外)。

花冠也采用了1.8升发动机。新内饰特点体现在丰田的气门技术以提高燃料效率和活塞功率达140马力。说到技术，四速自动仍然可见，但大多保留在销售的基本型L。所有其他的花冠将配备CVT，而基本型L和运动型S可以配六速手动。

标定一样，表现不同

燃油经济性是我们比较车辆的热点。思域EXL官方标定为城市28 mpg和公路39 mpg，而花冠S是城市29 mpg和公路37 mpg。但那是在纸上。在现实世界中出现了一个明显的赢家；花冠平均34.6 mpg，而思域只有33.1 mpg。

因仪表板和腰线低，思域四周视野较好，但有些高个驾驶员觉得座位偏高，相反，花冠仪表板高，对有些矮个驾驶员来说，前向视野较差。

花冠的反应感觉迟钝得多，因转向和节气门响应不是特别快，发动机与CVT的配对有点噪音，但车速调节很快，在运动模式可以通过七个模拟齿轮调节转速。

结论

思域起价18 995美元，比基本型花冠高1 385美元。全配带导航的思域EX－L最终价为24 922美元，而花冠S高配23 570美元。思域也有经销商安装17英寸车轮不包括在价格中，因此价格进一步上涨。

虽然思域在驱动方面稍有优势，消费者真正关心的是紧凑型轿车更实用的特征，如价格、燃油经济性和空间是他们优先考虑因素，花冠在这些方面比思域占优。在如此接近的比赛中，这已经足以确认它的胜利。

Unit 20

Best New Sedans of 2020

扫码获取
扩展视频

While sedans might not have the fun and flash of sports cars or SUVs, there are still many that are worthy of your consideration.

Sedans are a little like the dad jeans of the automotive world. While perhaps not always the most stylish of choices, they can be comfortable, practical, and come in sizes ranging from small to full-size. There are tons of options in the sedan category, but these are the best sedans you can buy today.

Those who are interested in the best sedans from 2019 can refer to last year's list.

The 2020 Yaris offers a lot more than you might expect from a budget-priced car. Available in hatchback and sedan body styles, this accomplished subcompact boasts the kind of exceptional fuel economy that can save you money over the long haul. Its suspension is tuned to facilitate driver engagement, and while it isn't the quickest at the track, it feels capable in everyday driving. On a less positive note, this Toyota offers fewer driver-assistance features than some rivals. Still, it all adds up to a value proposition that's extremely compelling for shoppers who have their sights set on a small car that's economically priced.

Fig. 20 - 1 Toyota Yaris

Fig. 20 - 2 Honda Civic

Few cars manage to satisfy everyone, but the 2020 Civic proves one car can be affordable and functional as well as entertaining. In our opinion, the Honda achieves a near perfect blend of comfort and driver engagement. Its steering responds immediately to driver inputs, its ride is smooth yet sporty, making it a blast to drive. The main drawback is its divisive exterior styling. Those who can appreciate or look past that aspect will enjoy its excellent fuel economy, copious interior cubby space, and numerous standard driver assists. It's one of the best compact sedans you can buy.

With comprehensive refinement and sophisticated driving manners, the 2020 Mazda 3 is one of the nicest compact cars in its class. Available as a hatchback or sedan, the Mazda is a richer-feeling alternative to rivals such as the Honda Civic and the Toyota Corolla . In our testing, its responsive four-cylinder engine proved frugal on the highway, and both body styles maintain Mazda's commitment to driver engagement. While the 3 doesn't offer a high-performance model, it's always agile when the tarmac curves and comfy when the road gets rough. An excellent infotainment system and standard driver assists place the 2020 Mazda 3 among the best compacts out there.

Fig. 20 - 3 Mazda 3

Fig. 20 - 4 Honda Accord

We've named the Accord to our 10 Best list a record number of times because it's perennially the most impressive family sedan on sale—and the 2020 model is no different. The Honda has three powertrain choices—including a hybrid—blend efficiency and power. Graceful handling is an Accord hallmark and its athletic chassis, lightly weighted steering, and balanced ride come standard across the lineup. Also standard: a suite of driver-assistance features including automated emergency braking, lane-keeping assist, and adaptive cruise control. The 2020 Accord is not only the best-driving family sedan, it's also one of the best-equipped choices in its class, making it an easy recommendation for today's car shoppers.

The iconic and perennially popular BMW 3-series remains one of the more dynamic luxury sedans available. The latest generation is the largest 3-series to date, and while some purists will complain it's not the pure sports sedan that it once was, it's still a thrill to drive with sharp handling, powerful and refined turbocharged engines, and a responsive automatic transmission. Although its exterior design is a bit conservative, the interior offers class-leading comfort, quality, and style.

Fig. 20 - 5 BMW 3-Series

NEW WORDS

sedan	[sɪˈdæn]	*n.*	轿车
consideration	[kənˌsɪdəˈreɪʃn]	*n.*	考虑
stylish	[ˈstaɪlɪʃ]	*adj.*	新潮的
subcompact	[ˈsʌbˈkɒmpækt]	*n.*	紧凑型汽车
hatchback	[ˈhætʃbæk]	*n.*	掀背式汽车
haul	[hɔːl]	*vt.*	拖;拉
proposition	[ˌprɑːpəˈzɪʃn]	*n.*	建议
entertaining	[ˌentəˈteɪnɪŋ]	*adj.*	有趣的
refinement	[rɪˈfaɪnmənt]	*n.*	改进;改善
powertrain	[ˈpaʊə·tren]	*n.*	传动系统
tarmac	[ˈtɑːrmæk]	*n.*	柏油碎石路面
frugal	[ˈfruːgl]	*adj.*	朴素的
iconic	[aɪˈkɒnɪk]	*adj.*	偶像的
perennially	[pəˈreniəli]	*adv.*	长期地
purist	[ˈpjʊrɪst]	*n.*	力求纯粹的人
hallmark	[ˈhɔːlmɑːrk]	*n.*	检验标记

REFERENCE TRANSLATION

2020年最佳家用轿车

虽然轿车可能没有跑车或SUV的乐趣和闪光之处,但仍有许多地方值得你考虑。

轿车有点像汽车界的老爹牛仔裤。虽然可能不总是最时尚的选择,但它们可以是舒适的,实用的,并有大小不等的小到全尺寸。在轿车类别中有很多选择,但这些是你今天能买到的最好的轿车。

对2019年以来最好的轿车感兴趣的人可以参考去年的榜单。

2020款雅力士提供了比你可能期望的预算价格的汽车更多的东西。该款车的车身可做成掀背式和轿车的风格,这一成功的超小型车还拥有一种出色的燃油经济性,可以为你节省钱,从长远来看。它的悬挂系统经过调整以便于驾驶员参与,虽然它在赛道上不是最快的,但它在日常驾驶中感觉很得力。一个不太积极的方面是,这款丰田提供的驾驶员辅助功能比一些竞争对手要少。不过,这一切加起来都是一种价值主张,对于那些将目光投向一辆价格经济的小型车的购物者来说,这是一个极具吸引力的价值主张。

很少有车能让所有人都满意,但2020款思域证明了一款车既能让人们负担得起,又能满足人们的娱乐需求。在我们看来,本田实现了舒适性和驾驶员参与度的近乎完美的融合。它的转向系统对驾驶员的操纵立即做出反应,它的行驶平顺而富有运动感,富有驾驶乐趣。它主要的缺点是其分裂的外观造型。那些能够欣赏或回顾这方面的人将享受其出色的燃油经济性、丰富的内部小隔间以及众多标准驾驶辅助系统。这是你能买到的最好的紧凑型轿车之一。

2020款马自达3是同级别中最漂亮的紧凑型车之一,拥有全面的精致配置和精细的驾驶方式。作为掀背式车或轿车,马自达是一个令人感觉更丰富的替代品,如替代本田思域和丰田花冠。在我们的测试中,它的反应灵敏的四缸发动机在高速公路上被证明是省油的,两种车身风格都保持了马自达对驾驶者参与度的承诺。虽然3并没有提供高性能的车型,但它在柏油路面转弯时总是很灵活,在路面崎岖不平的时候也很舒适。一个优秀的信息娱乐系统和标准的驾驶辅助将2020年马自达3列为最好的紧凑型车。

雅阁几次被评为2020年最畅销的十大车型之一,因为它是最受欢迎的车型之一,2020款也一样。本田有三种动力系统选择,包括混合动力——高效且动力强劲。优雅的操控是雅阁的一个标志,它的运动底盘,轻量化的方向盘,平衡的乘坐在整个阵容中都是标准配置。同时也是标准配置的是:一套驾驶员辅助功能,包括自动紧急制动、车道保持辅助和自适应巡航控制。2020款雅阁不仅是驾驶性能最好的家庭轿车,也是同级车中装备最好的选择之一,这使得它很容易就被推荐给买车人。

几近偶像和永远流行的宝马3系仍然是一个更具活力的豪华轿车。最新一代是迄今为止最大的3系车型,虽然一些纯粹主义者会抱怨它不再是曾经的纯运动轿车,但凭借犀利的操控性、强大而精致的涡轮增压发动机以及反应灵敏的自动变速器,驾驶起来还是让人兴奋不已。虽然它的外观设计有点保守,但是内部提供了一流的舒适、高品质和新颖性。

Unit 21

Chinese NEV Startups Gain Momentum

扫码获取
扩展视频

Nio, the New York-listed Chinese electric car startup, said it expects sales in the fourth quarter this year to hit a record number of around 17,000 vehicles. That is not a big number for established carmakers, but it means a doubling of Nio's deliveries in the same quarter of last year.

The goal is not a castle in the air, though. The startup gave the estimate after it released its financial results of the third quarter on Tuesday, in which it delivered 12,206 vehicles. "In view of the growing market demand for our competitive products, we are motivated to continuously elevate the production capacity to the next level," said Nio founder and CEO William Li.

Fig. 21 - 1 Nio-es8

In the past few months, the startup has revealed a new battery pack, which extends its vehicles' driving range by around 100 kilometers to over 600 kilometers, launched its battery swap service and updated driving-assist functions for its vehicles.

These moves, together with the overall rise in China's new energy vehicle segment, pushed Nio's performance higher.

Statistics from the China Association of Automobile Manufacturers show that electric car and plug-in hybrid sales in October totaled 160,000; up 104.5 percent year-on-year. Steven Feng, Nio's chief financial officer, said the company's vehicle margin increased to 14.5 percent in the third quarter, generating 4,267 million yuan in revenue.

Feng said it had achieved positive cash flow from operating activities for the second sequential quarter. Its cash and cash equivalents by the end of September totaled 22 billion yuan.

Based on the bright sales prospects, Li said Nio will rev up its production capacity to 7,500 vehicles a month from January.

He said the company's fourth vehicle, a sedan, is around the corner and its fifth vehicle is in development.

Nio is not alone. Xpeng and Lixiang, also known as Li Auto, are listed in the United States as well and saw positive growth in the third quarter.

Analysts said the three, which label themselves as premium brands, are winning over buyers from traditional ones like BMW and Audi, whose products are mainly gasoline vehicles.

Favorable government policies and license plate quotas for gasoline vehicles in big cities like Beijing have also helped their popularity, they said.

Fig. 21 – 2 automobile Xpeng-P7

Xpeng's total revenue from car sales in the third quarter reached 1,898 million yuan, up 376 percent from the same quarter last year. Its gross margin was 4.6 percent. In the second quarter, it was minus 2.7 percent.

He Xiaopeng, chairman and CEO of Xpeng, said the figures were mainly thanks to the fast rise in sales of the P7 sedan, the company's second model.

Statistics show that 6,210 P7 sedans were sold in the third quarter, accounting for 72.3 percent of its total deliveries in the quarter. Total deliveries went up 265.8 percent from the same quarter last year to reach 8,578.

By the end of September 30, Xpeng's cash and cash equivalents totaled almost 20 billion yuan. This ensures its investment in research and development, charging facilities, sales network and marketing, said He.

He estimated that Xpeng's deliveries in the fourth quarter could reach 10,000. He expected there will be around 150 dealerships by the end of the year.

Li Auto's financial results came out last week as well. It has only one model, and its deliveries reached 8,660 vehicles in the third quarter, up 31 percent from the second quarter. Its sales revenue totaled 2,465 million yuan, up 28.4 percent from the previous quarter.

By the end of the third quarter, it had cash and cash equivalents totaling 18.92 billion, up from 390 million late last year.

"We will further increase our investment and continue to leverage technology to create value for users and optimize our user experience," said Li Xiang, founder and CEO of Li Auto in a statement.

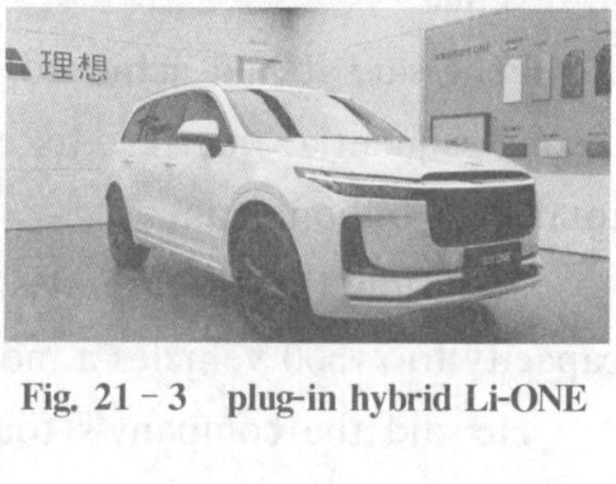

Fig. 21 – 3 plug-in hybrid Li-ONE

For the fourth quarter of 2020, Li Auto expected the growth momentum to continue in the fourth quarter, with deliveries reaching 11,000 to 12,000 vehicles.

NEW WORDS

momentum	[moʊ'mentəm]	*n.*	势头
startup	['stɑːtʌp]	*n.*	启动;新兴公司
motivate	['moʊtɪveɪt]	*vt.*	激励
reveal	[rɪ'viːl]	*vt.*	揭示透露
move	[muːv]	*n.*	行动
launch	[lɔːntʃ]	*vt.*	发布
margin	['mɑːrdʒɪn]	*n*	利润
swap	[swɑːp]	*n.*	交换
minus	['maɪnəs]	*prep.*	减去
investment	[ɪn'vestmənt]	*n.*	投资
revenue	['revənuː]	*n.*	年收入
previous	['priːviəs]	*adj.*	前一个
leverage	['levərɪdʒ]	*n.*	杠杆作用
iconic	[aɪ'kɑːnɪk]	*adj.*	偶像的

PHRASES

a castle in the air	空中楼阁
NEV	新能源汽车
plug-in hybrid	插电式混合动力汽车

REFERENCE TRANSLATION

中国新能源汽车创业势头强劲

在纽约上市的中国电动汽车初创企业 Nio 蔚来表示，预计今年第四季度的销量将达到创纪录的约 17 000 辆。对于老牌汽车制造商来说，这不是一个大数字，但这意味着 Nio 去年同期的交货量翻了一番。

不过，目标并不是空中楼阁。这家初创公司在周二公布了第三季度的财报后给出了这一估计，该财报共交付了 12 206 辆汽车。Nio 创始人兼首席执行官李威廉(William Li)表示："鉴于市场对我们竞争产品的需求不断增长，我们有动力不断提升生产能力至下一个水平。”

在过去的几个月里，这家初创公司推出了一种新的电池组，它将汽车的行驶里程延长了大约100公里至600多公里，并推出了电池更换服务，并为其车辆更新了驾驶辅助功能。

这些举措，加上中国新能源汽车板块的整体上涨，推动了蔚来的业绩走高。

来自中国汽车工业协会的统计数据显示，10月份电动汽车和插电式混合动力汽车的总销量为16万辆，同比增长104.5%。Nio首席财务官史蒂芬·冯(Steven Feng)表示，公司第三季度的汽车利润率增至14.5%，实现收入42.67亿元。

冯表示，该公司连续第二季度的经营活动现金流为正。截至9月底，公司现金及现金等价物共计220亿元。

基于光明的销售前景，李表示，从明年1月起，Nio将把产能提高到每月7 500辆。

他说，该公司的第四款车型轿车即将上市，第五款车型正在研发中。

蔚来并不孤单。小鹏和理想也被称为“理想汽车”，也在美国上市，并且在第三季度实现了正增长。

分析师表示，这三家标榜自己是高端品牌的汽车厂商正在争取宝马(BMW)和奥迪(Audi)等传统品牌的买家，后者的产品主要是汽油车。

他们说，在北京这样的大城市，政府的优惠政策和汽油车的牌照配额也有助于它们的普及。

小鹏第三季度汽车销售总收入达到18.98亿元，比去年同期增长376%。其毛利率为4.6%。在第二季度，这个数字是－2.7%。

小鹏董事长兼首席执行官何晓鹏表示，这些数据主要得益于公司第二款车型P7轿车销量的快速增长。

统计显示，第三季度P7轿车共销售6 210辆，占其一季度总交付量的72.3%。总交付量较去年同期增长265.8%，达到8 578架。

截至9月30日，小鹏现金及现金等价物总额近200亿元。他说，这确保了其在研发、充电设施、销售网络和营销方面的投资。

他估计，小鹏在第四季度的交货量可能达到1万台。他预计到今年年底将有150家左右的经销商。

理想汽车的财报也在上周公布。它只有一款车型，第三季度交付量达到8 660辆，比第二季度增长了31%。销售收入24.65亿元，比上季度增长28.4%。

截至第三季度末，该公司的现金及现金等价物总额为189.2亿美元，高于去年底的3.9亿美元。

“我们将进一步加大投入，继续利用技术为用户创造价值，优化用户体验，”理想汽车(Li Auto)创始人兼CEO李想在一份声明中表示。

对于2020年第四季度，理想汽车预计第四季度的增长势头将继续，交付量将达到1.1万辆至1.2万辆。

Unit 22

Tesla Model S: New Carbon Fiber
—Body Kit and Proof

扫码获取
扩展视频

I've been critical of electric cars, often bashing them for their lack of "soul". Stepping on the accelerator doesn't quite give the emotion I've been so accustomed to from a gasoline engine, especially those with turbochargers. EV cars honestly made me feel like I was inside an oversized, glorified golf cart, especially in their infancy. As the years went by, though, gas prices continue to climb and more interesting EV offerings have emerged beyond cars like the Chevy Bolt.

Today there are more than 15 new electric cars available at U.S. dealerships and charging stations are springing up like mushrooms in every major city—something that used to be a pain to locate. Sportier and more luxurious EV models are also getting into the hands of not just those looking to save the planet and cut their monthly gas bills, but enthusiasts who care about style and performance, which is the case for this 2019 Tesla Model S P100D.

TESLA AIN'T NO JOKE

I won't go too far in depth on the Tesla and its flagship Model S, but let's be fair... Since 2017, the Model S has been making headlines everywhere, whether you liked it or not. I was never a big fan of its rather boring design; however, the top-of-the-line P100D model has been outrunning any supercar or hypercar you can think of in a 0 - 60 mph dash in just 2.3 seconds (2.28 seconds as tested by Motor Trend). It's quite ludicrous (pun intended).

Tesla's overall AWD performance has also received some good feedback from the motorsports community as well. In 2018, Mountainpass Performance campaigned a modified Model 3 in time attack, which recorded a 2:00 lap time at Buttonwillow Raceway during the annual Super Lap Battle (seconds faster than Evos and STis in its class). Last year, Tesla released a Twitter video of a prototype Model

S lapping Laguna Seca Raceway in 1:36.555 (basically on par with a Nissan GT-R or Porsche 911). These are huge feats for a car manufacturer that hasn't even been around two decades yet. The Palo Alto-based company continues to gain momentum, not just with wealthy housewives and computer programmers, but with the enthusiast community. TDG is the latest player to jump into the EV game and they have some new and exciting parts that might pique your interest.

First things first about modifying electric cars: you don't really want to touch the electric motors (unless you're some sort of electrical engineering/computer programming genius). The Model S P100D already comes as a rocketship so what most logical tuners address are the suspension, brakes, grip, wheels, aero and weight reduction. TDG has developed two product lines for its Model S (which will fit all 2016.5 models and newer), which are the body kit and brake rotors.

The body kit is pretty straightforward, designed by Jon Sibal, made of 100% carbon fiber (not just an overlay), it includes the front lip, side skirts, rear diffuser and trunk spoiler. The entire package retails for $ 7,250.

The front and rear brake rotors have a bit more story behind them. Named "ULTRADISC", the rotors are slotted for better cooling; however, the biggest advantage comes from saving 22lbs. of unsprung weight when you change out all four rotors. This benefits the Tesla by improving handling, acceleration and braking, as well as reducing energy use. According to TDG, the reduction of unsprung weight is 8.4% resulting in almost 20 more miles of range.

Sharpening up the handling and further reducing body roll are KW coilovers. If you're privy to the Model S P100D, then you'll understand that TDG had to rip out the factory air ride suspension including the air compressor in order to install the coilovers. We imagine it's not what most Tesla owners would do, however, the TDG demo car is intended to be more of a track-capable sedan as opposed to a glorified grocery getter.

Last but not least are the Volk Racing TE37 wheels which, quite frankly, look damn good on just about anything. The stock Model S comes with 19-inch wheels and the loaded model comes with 21-inch wheels. TDG spec'd its TE37s at 20x9 "front and 20x10" rear with grippier NT05s, which is a much more aggressive tire than the OEM equipment. We have to say, with the combination of the carbon lip kit, RAYS wheels and lowered KW suspension, this Model S looks pretty damn proper and is easily one of the better looking modified Teslas we've seen.

NEW WORDS

fiber	[ˈfaɪbər]	*n.*	纤维
critical	[ˈkrɪtɪkl]	*adj.*	批评的
bash	[bæʃ]	*vt.*	猛击；严厉批评
accelerator	[əkˈseləreɪtər]	*n.*	油门踏板
turbocharger	[ˈtɜːrboʊtʃɑːrdʒər]	*n.*	涡轮增压器
infancy	[ˈɪnfənsi]	*n.*	婴儿期；初期
Chevy	[ˈtʃevi]	*n*	雪佛莱
enthusiast	[ɪnˈθuːziæst]	*n.*	狂热爱好者
flagship	[ˈflægʃɪp]	*n.*	旗舰；佼佼者
campaign	[kæmˈpeɪn]	*n.*	运动
feat	[fiːt]	*n.*	技艺；功绩
aggressive	[əˈgresɪv]	*adj.*	侵略的；有闯劲的
suspension	[səˈspenʃn]	*n.*	悬架
genius	[ˈdʒiːniəs]	*n.*	天才

PHRASES

lack of soul	缺少灵魂
as the years went by	随着时间的流逝
spring up like mushrooms	雨后春笋般出现

REFERENCE TRANSLATION

特斯拉 S 型车：新型碳纤维车身

我一直对电动汽车持批评态度，经常抨击电动汽车缺乏"灵魂"。踩油门并不能让我感受到习惯的汽油发动机，尤其是那些装有涡轮增压器的发动机。说实话，电动汽车让我感觉自己就像坐在一辆超大的、华丽的高尔夫球车里，尤其是在它们的发展初期。然而，随着时间的推移，汽油价格继续攀升，除了雪佛兰博尔特(chevybolt)这样的汽车之外，更多有趣的电动汽车产品也出现了。

如今，美国经销商处有超过 15 款新的电动汽车，充电站如雨后春笋般在每个大城市涌现，这在过去很难找到。更运动、更豪华的 EV 车型也进入了不仅仅是那些希望拯救地球、削减每月汽油费的人的手中，还有那些关心款式和性能的爱好者们，这就是这款 2019 年特斯拉 S P100D 车型的情况。

特斯拉不是开玩笑

我不会对特斯拉和它的旗舰车型 S 做太深入的探讨，但公平地说，2017 年以来，无论你喜不喜欢，S 型车就成了各地的头条新闻。我从来不迷恋它那相当无聊的设计；然而，顶级的 P100D 车型已经超过了任何一个超级跑车或超跑中的超跑，你可以想到在一个 0—60 英里/小时的冲刺在短短的 2.3 秒(2.28 秒，由汽车趋势测试)完成。这很可笑(双关语的意思)。

特斯拉的整体 AWD 表现也得到了一些来自赛车界的良好反馈。2018 年，Mountainpass Performance 推出了一款及时改进的 Model 3，在年度超级单圈大战中，记录了 Buttonwillow 赛道的 2:00 圈速(快于同级的 Evos 和 STI)。去年，特斯拉在 Twitter 上发布了一段视频，视频中原型车型 S 以 1 分 36 秒 555 的圈速位列第二名，擦过拉古纳赛卡赛道(基本上与日产 GT-R 或保时捷 911 不相上下)。对于一个还没有 20 年的汽车制造商来说，这些都是巨大的成就。这家总部位于帕洛阿尔托的公司继续获得发展势头，不仅在富有的家庭主妇和计算机程序员中，而且在爱好者社区中。TDG 是最新加入电动汽车游戏的玩家，他们有一些新的和令人兴奋的部分，可能会激起你的兴趣。

改装电动汽车首先要明白的事情是：你并不能真的去改装电动机(除非你是某种电气工程师/计算机编程天才)。SP100D 车型已经像宇宙飞船一样程序逻辑复杂，所以你能解决的只是悬挂、刹车、抓地力、车轮、空气动力和重量减轻。TDG 为其 S 型车开发了两条生产线(适用于所有 2016.5 及更新车型)，即车身套件和制动盘。

车身套件非常简单，由 Jon Sibal 设计，由 100%碳纤维制成(不仅仅是覆盖层)，它包括前唇板、侧裙板、后扰流器和后备厢扰流器。整个套餐的零售价为 7 250 美元。

前后刹车盘背后有更多的故事。名为“超级圆盘”的转子开槽，可以更好地冷却；然而，最大的优势是，当你更换所有四个转子时，可节省 22 磅的承重。这有利于特斯拉改善操控、加速和制动，以及减少能源消耗。据 TDG 称，承担重量减少了 8.4%，航程增加了近 20 英里。

提高操控性和进一步减少车身侧倾是 KW 的酷爱。如果你知道型号 S P100D，那么你就会明白，为了安装减震器，TDG 不得不拆掉工厂的空气悬架，包括空气压缩机。我们认为这不是大多数特斯拉车主会做的，然而，TDG 演示车是打算打造成具有更好的通行能力的轿车，而不是美化的买菜车。

最后，沃尔克赛车 TE37，坦率地说，它的任何东西看起来都非常好。库存车型 S 配备 19 英寸车轮，装载车型配备 21 英寸车轮。TDG 的规格是其 TE37s 在 20x9“前和 20x10”后方与抓地力 NT05s，这是一个比原始设备制造商的设备更有力的轮胎。我们不得不说，结合碳纤套件，光线车轮和低功耗悬架，这款 S 型车看起来非常合适，很容易成为我们见过的更好看的改装特斯拉之一。

Appendix

I Vocabulary

A

abbreviate	[ə'bri:vieɪt]	*vt.*	缩写
accelerate	[ək'seləreɪt]	*adj.*	加速
accumulator	[ə'kju:mjəleɪtə]	*n.*	集水器
ammeter	['æmi:tə]	*n.*	电表
announcement	[ə'naʊnsmənt]	*n.*	预告
antagonize	[æn'tægənaɪz]	*vt.*	引起……敌对
antifreeze	['æntifri:z]	*n.*	防冻液
armrest	['ɑ:mrest]	*n.*	(座位的)扶手
automatization	[ɔ:təmætɪ'zeɪʃən]	*n*	自动化
awry	[ə'raɪ]	*adj.*	错误的
axle	[æksl]	*n.*	轮轴,车轴

B

backlash	['bæklæʃ]	*n.*	反击
band	[bænd]	*n.*	制动带
bankruptcy	['bæŋkrʌptsi]	*n.*	破产
block	[blɔk]	*n.*	缸体
bog	[bɒg]	*vt.*	使不能前进
bonnet	['bɒnɪt]	*n.*	发动机盖
breaker	['breɪkə]	*n.*	断电器
browse	[braʊz]	*vt. & vi.*	随意翻阅
bumping	['bʌmpɪŋ]	*v.*	冲撞

C

cadre	['kɑ:də(r)]	*n.*	核心
camshaft	['kæmʃɑ:ft]	*n.*	凸轮轴
casualty	['kæʒuəlti]	*n.*	伤亡人员;事故车
chart	[tʃɑ:t]	*n.*	图表
chevrolet	['ʃevrəleɪ]	*n.*	雪佛兰牌汽车

chrome	[krəʊm]	*n*.	铬合金
click	[klɪk]	*n*.	滴答声
club	[klʌb]	*n*.	会员
clunker	[ˈklʌŋkə]	*n*.	破旧不堪的汽车
clutch	[klʌtʃ]	*n*.	离合器
coefficient	[ˌkəʊɪˈfɪʃnt]	*n*.	系数
collision	[kəˈliʒən]	*n*.	碰撞
commitment	[kəˈmɪtm(ə)nt]	*n*.	承诺
compressor	[kəmˈpresə]	*n*.	空气压缩机
condenser	[kənˈdensə]	*n*.	电容器;冷凝器
confuse	[kənˈfjuːz]	*v*.	使糊涂
conscious	[ˈkɒnʃəs]	*adj*.	有意识的
console	[kənˈsəʊl]	*n*.	控制台
conspire	[kənˈspaɪə(r)]	*vt*.	共谋
conundrum	[kəˈnʌndrəm]	*n*.	难题
conventional	[kənˈvenʃənl]	*adj*.	传统的
corrode	[kəˈrəʊd]	*vt*. & *vi*.	使腐蚀
corrosive	[kəˈrəʊsɪv]	*adj*.	腐蚀性的
crankshaft	[ˈkræŋkʃɑːft]	*n*.	曲轴
crate	[kreɪt]	*n*.	装货箱
credit	[ˈkredɪt]	*n*.	信用
cripple	[ˈkrɪpl]	*vt*.	使陷于瘫痪
criteria	[kraɪˈtɪərɪə]	*n*.	标准
criterion	[kraɪˈtɪəriən]	*n*.	标准
crosswalk	[ˈkrɒswɔːk]	*n*.	人行横道
curb	[kɜːb]	*n*.	路边
cuss	[kʌs]	*vt*.	咒骂
cyclist	[ˈsaɪklɪst]	*n*.	骑自行车的人
cylinder	[ˈsɪlɪndə]	*n*.	缸套

D

dashboard	[ˈdæʃbɔːd]	*n*.	仪表板
dealership	[ˈdiːləʃɪp]	*n*.	经销权
debtor	[ˈdetə(r)]	*n*.	债务人
decelerate	[diːˈseləreɪt]	*v*.	减速
defend	[dɪˈfend]	*vt*.	拒绝承认
dehumidification	[ˈdiːhjuːˌmɪdɪfɪˈkeɪʃən]	*n*.	除去湿气
demarcate	[ˈdiːmɑːkeɪt]	*vt*.	定……的界线

deplete	[di'pliːt]	*v*.	耗尽
depreciate	[dɪ'priːʃieɪt]	*vt*.	使贬值
desperately	['despərətli]	*adv*.	极度地
destination	[ˌdestɪ'neiʃn]	*n*.	目的地
detroit	[dɪ'trɔɪt]	*n*.	美国底特律
diesel	['diːzl]	*n*.	柴油机
differential	[ˌdɪfə'renʃl]	*n*.	差速器
dimple	[dɪmpl]	*n*.	旋涡
diode	['daɪəud]	*n*.	二极管
disc	[dɪsk]	*n*.	圆盘
disengage	[ˌdɪsɪn'geɪdʒ]	*vt*.	分开
disk	[disk]	*adj*.	盘式的
dispatch	[dɪ'spætʃ]	*vt*.	调度
distinct	[dis'tiŋkt]	*adj*.	不同的
doughnut	['dəunʌt]	*n*.	圆环
drab	[dræb]	*adj*.	单调的
drastic	['dræstɪk]	*adj*.	猛烈的
durability	[ˌdjuərɔ'bɪləti]	*n*.	耐久力

E

eerie	['ɪəri]	*adj*.	奇怪的
electromagnet	[ɪ'lektrəʊmægnət]	*n*.	电磁铁
electromechanical	[ɪˌlektrəʊmə'kænɪkəl]	*adj*.	机电的
eliminate	[ɪ'lɪmɪneɪt]	*vt*.	排除
emission	[ɪ'mɪʃn]	*n*.	排放
equation	[ɪ'kweɪʒn]	*n*.	方程式
equivalence	[ɪ'kwɪvələns]	*n*.	等值物
essentially	[ɪ'senʃəlɪ]	*adj*.	基本的
evaluate	[ɪ'væljueɪt]	*vt*.	评估
evaporator	[ɪ'væpəreɪtə]	*n*.	蒸发器
exorbitant	[ɪg'zɔːbɪtənt]	*adj*.	极高的

F

fahrenheit	['færənhait]	*n*.	华氏温度
fatality	[fə'tæləti]	*n*.	死亡(事故)
federal	['fedərəl]	*adj*.	联邦(制)的
financial	[faɪ'nænʃl]	*adj*.	金融的
flange	[flændʒ]	*n*.	法兰盘
flywheel	['flaɪwiːl]	*n*.	飞轮

forensic	[fə'rensɪk]	*n.*	司法鉴定
forgo	[fɔː'gəʊ]	*vt. & vi.*	放弃
fray	[freɪ]	*v.*	磨损
freight	[freɪt]	*n.*	货运列车
	G		
gage	[geɪdʒ]	*n.*	压力计
gallon	['gælən]	*n.*	加仑
gap	['gæp]	*n.*	间隙
garage	['gærɑː(d)ʒ]	*n.*	车库
genuine	['dʒenjuɪn]	*adj.*	真诚的
glove	[glʌv]	*n.*	手套
goggle	['gɒgl]	*n.*	护目镜
governor	['gʌvənə]	*n.*	调节器
grocery	['grəusəri]	*n.*	食品杂货店
	H		
herein	[ˌhɪər'ɪn]	*adv.*	在这里
holistic	[hə'lɪstɪk]	*adj.*	功能整体性的
horn	[hɔːn]	*n.*	喇叭
	I		
ideal	[aɪ'diːəl]	*adj.*	理想的
ignore	[ɪg'nɔː]	*vt.*	忽视
illumination	[ɪˌluːmɪ'neiʃn]	*n.*	闪烁
imperceptible	[ˌɪmpə'septəbl]	*adj.*	觉察不到的
incentive	[ɪn'sentɪv]	*n.*	刺激
indicator	['ɪndɪkeɪtə(r)]	*n.*	指示灯
induce	[ɪn'djuːs]	*v.*	引诱
inertia	[ɪ'nɜːʃə]	*n.*	惯性
inhibit	[ɪn'hɪbɪt]	*v.*	抑制、约束
injection	[ɪn'dʒekʃn]	*n.*	喷射
insulate	['ɪnsjuleɪt]	*v.*	隔离
intake	['ɪnteɪk]	*n.*	进气
integrate	['ɪntɪgreɪt]	*vt.*	集成
intermittent	[ˌɪntə'mɪtənt]	*adj.*	间歇的
interrupt	[ˌɪntə'rʌpt]	*vt.*	中断
irreparable	[ɪ'repərəbl]	*adj.*	不能修复的
	J		
jug	[dʒʌg]	*n.*	壶

L

labor	[ˈleɪbə(r)]	*n.*	劳工
lag	[læg]	*n.*	落后
lambaste	[læmˈbeɪst]	*vt.*	严责
landmark	[ˈlændmɑːk]	*n.*	里程碑
lane	[leɪn]	*n.*	车道
lateral	[ˈlætərəl]	*a.*	侧向的
leak	[liːk]	*vi.*	漏出
legroom	[ˈlegruːm]	*n.*	供伸腿的空间
loan	[loʊn]	*n.*	贷款
longitudinally	[ləndʒɪˈtjuːdɪnəli]	*adv.*	纵向的

M

magnetic	[mægˈnetɪk]	*adj.*	磁电式
malfunction	[mælˈfʌŋkʃn]	*n.*	故障
maneuver	[məˈnuːvə]	*n.*	策略
manual	[ˈmænjʊəl]	*n.*	手册
manufacture	[ˌmænjuˈfæktʃə]	*n.*	制造商
match	[mætʃ]	*v.*	匹配
mechanic	[məˈkænɪk]	*n.*	技工，机修工
mileage	[ˈmaɪlɪdʒ]	*n.*	里程数
milestone	[ˈmaɪlstəʊn]	*n.*	里程碑
minor	[ˈmaɪnə(r)]	*adj.*	少量的
misnomer	[ˈmisˈnəumə]	*n.*	用错名字
mixture	[ˈmɪkstʃə]	*adj.*	混合气
modulate	[ˈmɒdjuleɪt]	*vt.*	调整
moisture	[ˈmɔistʃə]	*n.*	潮湿、湿气
monsoon	[ˌmɒnˈsuːn]	*n.*	印度洋季风
motorist	[ˈməʊtərɪst]	*n.*	开汽车的人
municipal	[mjuːˈnɪsɪpl]	*adj.*	市政的

N

nameplate	[ˈneɪmpleɪt]	*n.*	商标
negotiate	[nɪˈgəʊʃieɪt]	*vt.*	谈判
neutral	[ˈnjuːtrəl]	*n./adj.*	空挡

O

obstacle	[ˈɒbstəkl]	*n.*	障碍(物)
occupant	[ˈɒkjəpənt]	*n.*	占有人
optimum	[ˈɒptɪməm]	*adj.*	最优的

organisation	[ˌɔːgənaɪˈzeɪʃn]	*n.*	组织
outsource	[ˈaʊtsɔːs]	*vt.*	外包(工程)
overhead	[ˈəuvəhed]	*adj.*	顶置的
ozone	[ˈəʊzəʊn]	*n.*	[化]臭氧

P

patrol	[pəˈtrəʊl]	*vt.*	巡逻
pavement	[ˈpeɪvmənt]	*n.*	公路
pedal	[ˈpedl]	*n.*	踏板
pedestrian	[pəˈdestriən]	*n.*	行人
penalty	[ˈpenəlti]	*n.*	惩罚
per	[pəː]	*prep.*	每;按照
perpendicular	[ˌpɜːpənˈdɪkjələ(r)]	*adj.*	垂直的
pinion	[ˈpinjən]	*n.*	小齿轮
planetary	[ˈplænətri]	*n.*	行星
pragmatic	[prægˈmætɪk]	*adj.*	实用主义的
preliminary	[prɪˈlɪmɪneri]	*adj.*	初步的
pretend	[priˈtend]	*vt.*	假装
procrastinate	[prəˈkræstɪneɪt]	*vi.*	拖延
prone	[prəʊn]	*adj.*	易于……的
puddle	[ˈpʌdl]	*vt.*	搅拌
puff	[pʌf]	*vt.*	喷出
pulsation	[pʌlˈseɪʃn]	*n.*	跳动、震动
pump	[pʌmp]	*n.*	泵
purchase	[ˈpəːtʃəs]	*n.*	购买

R

radically	[ˈrædɪkli]	*adv.*	完全地
refrigerant	[rɪˈfrɪdʒərənt]	*n.*	制冷剂
refund	[ˈriːfʌnd]	*n.*	退款
relevance	[ˈreləvəns]	*n.*	关联
relevant	[ˈreləvənt]	*adj.*	有关的
reliability	[rɪˌlaɪəˈbɪləti]	*n.*	可靠性
retrofit	[ˈretrəˌfit]	*v.*	翻新
retrofit	[ˈretrəufɪt]	*n.*	花样翻新
reverse	[rɪˈvəːs]	*vt. & vi.*	(使)反转
rival	[ˈraɪvl]	*n.*	对手
roadway	[ˈrəʊdweɪ]	*n.*	道路

S

saddle	[ˈsædl]	*n.*	鞍,鞍状物
saturation	[ˌsætʃəˈreɪʃn]	*n.*	磁饱和
savvy	[ˈsævi]	*adj.*	有见识的
sawdust	[ˈsɔːdʌst]	*n.*	木屑
scenario	[səˈnɑːriəu]	*n.*	情况
scheme	[skiːm]	*n.* & *v.*	技术,方案
scramble	[ˈskræmbl]	*vt.*	争夺
sculpt	[skʌlpt]	*vt.*	雕刻
seal	[siːl]	*n.*	密封
secondary	[ˈsekənderi]	*n.*	次级
sedan	[sɪˈdæn]	*n.*	〈美语〉小轿车
sedentary	[ˈsedntri]	*adj.*	久坐的
segment	[ˈsegmənt]	*n.*	部分
series	[ˈsɪəriːz]	*v.*	串联
severe	[sɪˈvɪə]	*adj.*	剧烈的
shallow	[ˈʃæləu]	*adj.*	浅的
shift	[ʃɪft]	*vi.*	换挡
shovel	[ˈʃʌvl]	*n.*	铲子
showroom	[ˈʃəuruːm]	*n.*	展厅
shrunk	[ʃrʌŋk]	*v.*	(使)缩水
sightline	[ˈsaɪtlaɪn]	*n.*	视线
skyrocket	[ˈskaɪrɒkɪt]	*vi.*	猛涨
slice	[slaɪs]	*vt.*	一部分
slippery	[ˈslɪpəri]	*adj.*	滑的
slope	[sləup]	*vi.*	有斜度
soak	[səuk]	*vt.*	吸入
solenoid	[ˈsəulənɒɪd]	*n.*	电磁开关
specification	[ˌspesɪfɪˈkeɪʃn]	*n.*	参数
spectacle	[ˈspektəkl]	*adj.*	现场的
spill	[spɪl]	*n.*	溢出量
spot	[spɒt]	*n.*	地点
squeal	[skwiːl]	*v.*	发出尖叫
squeeze	[skwiːz]	*vt.*	挤压
stall	[stɔːl]	*vt.* & *vi.*	(使)熄火
stator	[ˈsteitə]	*n.*	导轮
streetcar	[ˈstritˌkɑr]	*n.*	有轨电车

strive	[straɪv]	*v*.	努力
stroke	[strəuk]	*n*.	冲程
stylish	[ˈstaɪlɪʃ]	*adj*.	流行的
suburban	[səˈbɜːbən]	*adj*.	郊外的
suspension	[səˈspenʃn]	*n*.	悬架
switch	[swɪtʃ]	*n*.	开关
switchgear	[ˈswɪtʃˌɡɪə]	*n*.	接电装置
symphony	[ˈsɪmfəni]	*n*.	交响乐
synchronize	[ˈsɪŋkrənaɪz]	*n*.	同步

T

tackle	[ˈtækl]	*vt*.	处理
tailor	[ˈteɪlə]	*n*.	裁缝
terminal	[ˈtəːminl]	*v*.	端子
terminology	[ˌtəːmiˈnɔlədʒi]	*n*.	术语
theoretical	[θiəˈretɪkl]	*adj*.	理论上的
throttle	[ˈθrɒtl]	*n*.	节流阀
tip	[tɪp]	*n*.	小窍门
tire	[ˈtaɪə]	*n*.	轮胎
torque	[tɔːk]	*n*.	转矩
traction	[ˈtrækʃn]	*n*.	牵引力
transformer	[trænsˈfɔːmə(r)]	*n*.	变压器
transition	[trænˈziʒən]	*n*.	转变
traverse	[trəˈvɜːs]	*n*.	横越 穿过
trumps	[trʌmp]	*n*.	喇叭
turbine	[ˈtəːbin, -bain]	*n*.	涡轮
turn	[təːn]	*n*.	匝数
tutorial	[tjuːˈtɔːrɪəl]	*n*.	使用说明书
tweak	[twiːk]	*vt*.	用力拉

U

undiminished	[ˌʌndɪˈmɪnɪʃt]	*adj*.	未减少的
union	[ˈjuːniən]	*n*.	联盟
unveil	[ˌʌnˈveɪl]	*vt*.	使公之于众
urbanlization	[ˌɜːbənaɪˈzeɪʃn]	*n*.	都市化

V

vacuum	[ˈvækjuːm]	*n*.	真空
valve	[vælv]	*n*.	阀
vaporize	[ˈveɪpəraɪz]	*v*.	汽化

version	[ˈvɜːʃn]	*n.*	版本
versus	[ˈvɜːsəs]	*prep.*	与……相对
vibration	[vaɪˈbreɪʃn]	*v. & n.*	振动
voltage	[ˈvəʊltɪdʒ]	*n.*	电压
vulnerable	[ˈvʌlnərəbl]	*adj.*	易受伤的

V

wagon	[ˈwægən]	*n.*	四轮马车
webbing	[ˈwebɪŋ]	*n.*	带子
winch	[wɪntʃ]	*n.*	绞车
windshield	[ˈwɪndʃiːld]	*n.*	〈美〉汽车挡风玻璃
wiper	[ˈwaɪpə(r)]	*n.*	雨刷
wrecker	[ˈrekə(r)]	*n.*	救援清障

II The Names of Cars

德国			
BMW	宝马	Mercedes-Benz	奔驰
Opel	欧宝	VW	大众
Audi	奥迪	Porsche	保时捷
瑞典			
SAAB	绅宝	Volvo	沃尔沃
法国			
Citroen	雪铁龙	Renault	雷诺
Peugeot	标致		
西班牙			
SEAT	喜悦		
美国			
G. M.	通用	Buick	别克
Cadillac	凯迪拉克	Chevrolet	雪佛兰
Oldsmobile	奥斯摩比	Pontiac	庞帝克
Saturn	钍星	Mercury	水星
Ford	福特	Lincon	林肯
Chrysler	克莱斯勒	Jeep	吉普

续表

英国			
Rover	路宝	Jaguar	积架
Lotus	莲花	Rolls-Royce	劳斯莱斯
Aston Martin	奥斯顿马汀	Bentley	本特利
意大利			
Alfa	阿尔法	Lancia	兰吉雅
FIAT	菲亚特	Maserati	马莎拉帝
Ferrari	法拉利	Lamborghini	兰博基尼
Bugatti	伯嘉帝		
俄罗斯			
Lada	拉达		
日本			
Yelong	裕隆	Toyota	丰田
Honda	本田	Mitsubishi	三菱
Mazda	马自达	Daihatsu	大发
Suzuki	铃木	Subaru	速霸陆
Isuzu	五十铃	Nissan	尼桑
Eunos	优娜斯	Efini	仪飞尼
韩国			
Hyundai	现代	Daewoo	大宇
Kia	起亚	Ssang Yong	双阳

III The Lights and Instruments

AIR CLEANER 空气滤清器阻塞警示器
BEAM 前照灯远光指示灯
BELT 乘员座椅安全带警示灯
CHARGE 蓄电池充电指示灯
DOOR 车门警示灯
EXHBRAKE 排气制动指示灯
FILTER 柴油滤清器警示灯
FUEL 燃油表
GLOW 预热指示灯
LIGHTS 灯光故障警示灯

ODOMETER	里程表
SPEEDOMETER	车速表
T.BELT	正时或同步皮带指示灯
TACHOMETER	发动机转速表
TEMP	水温表
TRIPMETER	单程里程计
VAC	真空警示灯
WATER	发动机冷却液液位警示灯

IV The Abbreviation

缩 写	英文含义	中文含义
A/C	Air Conditioning	空调
AT	Automatic Transmission	自动变速器
ACC	Air Condition Clutch	空调离合器
ACT	Air Charge Temperature	进气温度
AFC	Air Flow Control	空气流量控制
AFS	Air Flow Sensor	空气流量传感器
AI	Air Injection	二次空气喷射
ACL	Air Cleaner	空气滤清器
ALT	Alternator	交流发电机
AP	Accelerator Pedal	油门踏板
ABS	Anti-lock Brake System	防抱死系统
A/F	Air Fuel Ratio	空燃比
B+	Battery Positive Voltage	蓄电池正极
C3I	Computer Controlled Coil Ignition	计算机控制点火
CAT	Catalytic Convertor	触媒转换器
CPU	Central Processing Unit	中央处理器
DLC	Data Link Connector	数据传递插接器
DTC	Diagnostic Trouble Code	诊断故障码
EFI	Electronic Fuel Injection	电控燃油喷射
EGR	Exhaust Gas Recirculation Valve	废气再循环
L/C	Lock-Up Clutch	锁止离合器
LED	Light Emitting Diode	发光二极管
MAF	Mass Air Flow Sensor	空气流量传感器

续表

缩　写	英文含义	中文含义
SRS	Supplemental Restraint System	安全气囊
VSS	Vehicle Speed Sensor	汽车速度传感器
VSV	Vacuum Solenoid Valve	真空电磁阀
VVIS	Variable Volume Intake System	可变进气系统

参考文献

1. 蔡北勤.汽车专业英语(第二版)[M].北京:清华大学出版社,2017.
2. 宋进桂.汽车专业英语(第二版)[M].北京:机械工业出版社,2019.
3. 关云霞.汽车专业英语(第二版)[M].北京:电子工业出版社,2015.
4. 王海琳.汽车专业英语(第二版)[M].北京:机械工业出版社,2017.
5. 黄韶炯.汽车专业英语(第三版)[M].北京:人民交通出版社,2018.
6. 张经柱.汽车工程专业英语(第二版)[M].北京:化学工业出版社,2019.
7. 杜文贤,刘凤波.汽车专业英语[M].北京:化学工业出版社,2019.
8. 卢晓春.汽车专业英语[M].北京:机械工业出版社,2018.